THE
SOCIOPATHIC
PERSONALITY

THE SOCIOPATHIC PERSONALITY

By **Benjamin B. Wolman**

BRUNNER/MAZEL *Publishers* • New York

The excerpts on pp. 47–48, 87–94, 123–125, 139–141, and 177–179 are reprinted with permission as follows:

Charles R. Keith, M.D. (Ed.), *The Aggressive Adolescent*, copyright © 1984 by The Free Press, a Division of Macmillan, Inc., New York.

American Psychiatric Association, *Diagnostic and Statistical Manual of Mental Disorders, Third Edition*, copyright © 1980 by APA, Washington, DC.

Library of Congress Cataloging-in-Publication Data

Wolman, Benjamin B.
    The sociopathic personality.

    Bibliography: p. 185
    Includes indexes.
    1. Antisocial personality disorders. I. Title.
[DNLM: 1. Antisocial Personality Disorder. WM 190 W865s]
RC555.W65   1987   616.85'82   86-26363
ISBN 0-87630-453-6

Copyright © 1987 by Benjamin B. Wolman

Published by
BRUNNER/MAZEL, INC.
19 Union Square
New York, New York 10003

All rights reserved. No part of this book may be reproduced by any process whatsoever without the written permission of the copyright owner.

MANUFACTURED IN THE UNITED STATES OF AMERICA

Contents

Preface vii

PART I: ETIOLOGY
    1. Genetic Determinants 5
    2. Neurological and
       Biochemical Determinants 11
    3. Sociocultural Determinants 17
    4. Parent-Child Interaction 23

PART II: SYMPTOMATOLOGY
    5. The Narcissistic-Parasitic Personality .. 39
    6. Aggressive and Violent Behavior 49
    7. Antisocial Behavior in
       Childhood and Adolescence 67
    8. Juvenile Delinquency 73

PART III: THEORETICAL VIEWPOINTS
    9. Psychiatric Manuals and
       Other Theories 87
   10. Psychoanalysis and Related Systems .. 98
   11. Learning Theories 104

12. Hyperinstrumental-Narcissistic
    Interpretation 108

PART IV: DIAGNOSTIC AND TREATMENT METHODS
13. Diagnosing Sociopathic Personality.... 121
14. Neuropharmacological Treatment 137
15. Psychoanalysis and Related Methods .. 142
16. Behavior Modification and
    Related Methods 146
17. Interactional Psychotherapy 153
18. Family and Group Therapies 162
19. Residential Treatment 170
20. The Road to Life 180

Bibliography 185
Name Index 195
Subject Index 198
About the Author 201

Preface

Antisocial and violent behavior is certainly on a rise. One cannot ignore the mushrooming of terrorist gangs who use wanton violence "in the name" of some allegedly lofty ideals, and the growing incidence of plain crime that represents a threat to the lives of innocent men, women, and children. Not all antisocial and self-righteous individuals are sociopaths, but all sociopaths are antisocial and self-righteous.

Democracy means "the same amount of freedom for all." Antisocial individuals practice "all freedom for themselves," at the expense of the rights of everyone else, and their selfish and antisocial behavior represents a threat to the democratic social order and to the security and often survival of peaceful citizens.

Is sociopathy a biological or sociopsychological phenomenon? The first part of this book analyzes the genetic, neurological and biochemical, sociocultural, and intrafamilial causal factors. The second part of the book describes the symptoms of sociopathy, namely, the narcissistic-parasitic patterns, the violent acting-out, the violent behavior in childhood, and juvenile delinquency. Part three of the book deals with the various theoretical approaches, represented by the psychiatric-diagnostic manuals, and the psychoanalytic, behavioristic, and hyperinstrumental interpretations. The fourth part describes the diagnostic and treatment methods, including neuropharmacology, psychoanalysis, behavior modification, interactional psychotherapy, family and group therapies, residential treatment, and, finally, a broad social approach called "the road to life."

Let me take the opportunity to express my profound gratitude for their most efficient and cordial cooperation to my editorial assistant, Morrell G. Binkley, and my research assistant, Susan B. Friedman.

June 1986   Benjamin B. Wolman

PART I

Etiology

1

Genetic Determinants

GENETIC RESEARCH

Genetic research underwent far-reaching changes in our times. In Freud's time genetics was mainly related to Mendel's laws of dominance and recessivity. The general belief was in 48 chromosomes linked in an unchangeable order in pairs. It was told that when Freud was asked about the role of genetics in etiology of mental disorders, his answer was "Disturbed parents have a shorter way to their children; they do not need genes."

At the present time, it is a well-known fact that human beings have 46 chromosomes, not 48. The chromosomes are not always paired; they may be three (trisomes) instead of two in a pair and sometimes they split. A gamut of chemical conglomerations of DNA and RNA can produce a variety of genetic features and an unlimited number of different geno- and phenotypes. When one sperm fertilizes one egg, there are eight million possible combinations of genes.

Moreover, similar symptoms can be produced by different physical and mental causes; thus the distinction between organic and nonorganic disorders has become exceedingly complex. Take, for instance, infantile autism; is it organic or psychogenic? My answer is "both," for I had the opportunity to see autistic children of both types. The symptoms of both types were almost identical despite totally different organic or psychological etiologies (Wolman, 1976).

A brief review of some research data will point to the difficulty in assessing the etiology of the sociopathic or psychopathic personality (I am using these two terms interchangeably). In the 1940s, I cooperated with the neuropsychiatrist Julius Moses in research on mongolism (Down syndrome). We related this syndrome to the mother's age, and we were totally wrong. In 1959 Lejeune, Gautier, and Turpin discovered an abnormal triplicate *(trisomy)* instead of a duplicate in the twenty-first chromosome pair. This abnormal *autosomal* phenomenon is definitely the cause of the Down syndrome. There are, however, Down syndrome cases related not to the trisomy but to *translocation*, that is, to a rare occurrence, when parts of broken chromosomes join a certain chromosomal pair.

At the present time we know that the *Klinefelter syndrome* is caused by abnormalities in the gametes. The genotype structure in Klinefelter syndrome is XXY, which results in a phenotype of a male with male genital organs, but lacking secondary sex characteristics. This genotype structure results also in mental retardation. Furthermore, *Tay-Sachs disease (amaurotic familial idiocy)* is transmitted by an autosomal recessive gene. The symptoms begin as early as the first year of life and include severely retarded mental development, disturbances of vision, convulsions, cherry-red macula, and muscular weakness.

At the present time, scientists have become more and more aware of the role of genetics in mental health and mental disorders. Certain abnormalities in the sex chromosomes may cause various maladaptive symptoms. In normal human males, the sex chromosome is XY and in normal human females XX, but chromosome abnormalities may appear among mentally retarded individuals as well as in the general population. Apparently, gametal abnormalities can be related to a variety of maladjusted phenomena. Psychosexual identity plays an important role in the development of one's sense of identity and overall adjustment. It is not known whether homosexual tendencies are related to chromosomal abnormalities, but hermaphroditism and transsexual transition from one sex to another create considerable adjustment difficulties (Wolman & Money, 1980).

GENETICS AND SOCIOPATHY

A study of 766 pairs of twins (Hare & Schalling, 1978) reported 55% concordance for antisocial, criminal behavior for identical, monozygotic twins as compared to 13% concordance for fraternal, dizygotic twins. Another study reported in the same volume points to the .70 correlation in hereditary criminal behavior in identical twins (MZ) and .28 correlation in nonidentical twins (DZ).

Also, research in adoption supports the hypothesis of genetic factors in sociopathy (Crowe, 1974, 1975). Of course, genetic predisposition is not the sole determinant of antisocial behavior, but practically all studies point to a higher correlation between the sociopaths and their biological parents than their adoptive parents (Mednick & Christiansen, 1980).

O'Neal et al. (1962) concluded their 30-year follow-up study of 524 sociopaths as follows:

1) A 30-year follow-up study of 524 patients originally seen in a child guidance clinic yielded a high proportion (20%) of former patients who met criteria for a diagnosis of sociopathic personality as adults, as compared with a control group (2%). The 84 male patients with this diagnosis are compared, with respect to their parents' behavior problems, to male patients with other psychiatric diseases (166) and to male patients diagnosed as having no disease (75).
2) Most patients who met the criteria for a diagnosis of sociopathic personality at any time during their adult lives still showed marked antisocial behavior up to time of follow-up (ages 31–54). For those in whom there was a marked diminution

of symptoms, this most often occurred between the ages of 30 and 35. There was no age, however, beyond which one did not improve.
3) Various forms of parental behavior that could be considered rejection were investigated. No form of rejection specifically directed at the child was found to be associated with the development of sociopathic personality, if the child's provocative behavior is taken into account. Desertion, failure to supervise, and nonsupport were found to be positively associated with the disease. Father's coldness was found to be negatively associated.
4) Parents with a history of divorce were more likely to have sociopathic children than parents without divorce.
5) A picture of generalized antisocial behavior in the father, suggesting a diagnosis of sociopathic personality, or alcoholism, was found to be related to sociopathic personality in the child. Whether or not children had actually lived with such fathers did not significantly affect their eventual rate of sociopathic personality.

HAMMER AND ANVIL

For a while there was a widely shared belief that antisocial behavior is related to an extra Y chromosome, and that men with XYY chromosomes are genetically inclined to antisocial, violent behavior. There is some evidence that the genotype XYY is correlated with tallness and low mentality, but there is no evidence that XYY or XXY predisposes one to violence. Witkin et al. (1976) studied 31,000 men born in Denmark in the years 1944–1947. Finally, of the 4,139 men investigated, 12 had an extra Y chromosome and 16 men had an extra X chromosome and were Klinefelter's cases. Three other males had some Y-chromosome translocations and were also included in the individual case study, which was then comprised of 31 chromosome-aberrant males. For each of these, two control subjects were matched on a number of demographic variables and on body height. One of the control subjects was matched on IQ. Ultimately 93 men participated in an examination of various cognitive abilities in a psychosocial interview and in a study of EEG, evoked potentials, and psychophysiology. The results of this study did not prove a clear causal relation between Y chromosome and sociopathy.

The relative role of genetics and environmental factors is still an open question. Some time ago a 15-year-old girl was brought to my office for consultation. The girl's mind was wandering. For a while she talked in a reasonable manner, but a few minutes later she was hallucinating. She mentioned that she knew me, that she had visited my office on several occasions, and asked me why I had changed my name. Apparently, the girl was schizophrenic, but her sister was rather well adjusted. The parents maintained that they treated both daughters in exactly the same manner; obviously, this was impossible, but, assuming a far-reaching similarity in environmental influences, one must look for genetic factors. Whatever wrong the parents did might be compared to blows of a hammer on an anvil. The hammer represents parental actions, the anvil represents the genetic predisposition. The blows of a hammer against a genetically sturdy predisposition of one girl have caused little if any harm, but the same blows against a genetically weak predisposition have caused serious damage.

Moreover, the more serious the genetically abnormal predisposition, the lesser the amount of stress necessary to produce maladjustment. People exposed to the same degree of environmental stress do not react the same way, for those whose innate traits are healthy may take much more hardship and frustration than those whose genotype is already affected.

Two children with the same genetic predisposition may ultimately develop as two different personalities if exposed to different environmental, physical, and psychosocial influences. Many a child may swallow lead, contract meningitis, or suffer brain injury and become severely handicapped. No less serious are social and psychological traumatic experiences that may adversely affect the mental health of a genetically healthy child, but less severe blows of a hammer can cause more serious damage to a genetically unhealthy child.

2

Neurological and Biochemical Determinants

NEUROLOGICAL STUDIES

The role of neurological and biochemical factors in human adjustment can hardly be overestimated. More than two thousand years ago, in ancient Greece, Hippocrates (460–370 B.C.) linked human behavior to four bodily fluids, namely, blood, phlegm, black bile, and yellow bile. These four fluids, called humors, were believed to be decisive determinants of human personality and behavior.

In the nineteenth century psychiatry was an integral part of neurology. People who suffered behavioral disturbances were called "nervous," for at that time all mental disorders were believed to originate in the nervous system.

Psychiatrists distinguished between two types of mental disorders, "organic" and "functional." Whenever there was evidence that a particular disorder was caused by genetic or by physicochemical environmental factors such as poisoning or infection, the disorder was called "organic." Whenever there was no proof for organicity, the disorder was labeled "functional." Fifty years ago, when I took my first course in psychopathology, the professor announced that *all* mental disorders are organic, and whenever the research does not prove their organicity, they are temporarily called functional. Hopefully, future research will prove that all disorders are caused by neurological or biochemical factors linked to genetics or to noxious environmental factors.

At the present time the relative role of neurology and biochemical factors is neither uncritically accepted nor uncritically rejected. It seems quite feasible that "many clinical features of sociopathy can be produced by the brain" (Reid, 1978, p. 146).

Antisocial and violent behavior is often associated with seizure disorders, alcohol and drug intoxication, and certain types of dementia, but none of these disorders is necessarily related to sociopathic personality. Car accidents may cause a decrease in mental abilities with the individual retaining mental alertness, and dementias can lead to rage and violence. The fact that sociopathic disorder could be related to neurological and biochemical causes does not justify lumping together all types of antisocial behavior under the name of sociopathy, whether all these cases are organic or sociogenic.

In his early work in comparative neurology, Pribram (1958) pointed to the connection between irritability and lack of sense of direction (typical for sociopathic behavior) and prefrontal lobotomy. Also, Hare (1975) noticed distinct neurological abnormalities in sociopaths, such as cortical hyperarousals and disturbance of reticular mechanisms, especially the diencephalic and mesencephalic mechanisms.

Goldstone (1983) related sociopathy to *maturational retardation*. Narcissism, impulsiveness, and inability to postpone gratification are usual signs of immaturity. The fact that the incidence of sociopathic antisocial behavior tends to decrease with age could support the hypothesis of maturational retardation and, specifically, slow cortical maturation.

Sociopaths tend to have low levels of resting skin conductance and less specific galvanic skin response, which could be indicative of a low level of arousal (Cleckley, 1976; Goldstone, 1983; Hare, 1970, 1975).

According to Eysenck (1964), sociopaths have a constitutional predisposition to rapid development of cortical inhibitions. They tend to learn slowly and forget quickly, and their behavior is not controlled by an adequate reasoning process.

However, despite a good deal of research, there is no final proof of neurological origins of sociopathy. Electrocortical investigations of sociopathy have failed, so far, to discover consistent relationships between sociopathic personality and cortically evoked potentials. As mentioned above, violent behavior can be caused by brain damage, temporal lobe dysfunction, psychomotor seizures, and other forms of epilepsy (Pincus, 1981) and may not be related to sociopathy.

Hare (1970, 1978) and others have reported slow-wave activity on EEG of sociopathic individuals, but it is not clear whether their slow wave significantly deviates from normal speed. Thus the connection between EEG data and sociopathy is still a possibility but lacks evidence.

Research of heart rate responses and other aspects of cardiovascular activity failed to discover any significant correlations between sociopathy and the cardiovascular system.

ENDOCRINOLOGICAL DATA

It has been a widespread belief that males are aggressive and females passive. Similar ideas were promoted by some psychoanalytic writers and many others. Some authors related the alleged male aggressiveness to testosterone (Mendelson, 1977), but research did not support this hypothesis. Some XYY-genotype males may have a somewhat higher incidence of violent behavior, but they do not necessarily have a higher level of testosterone (Brown & Goodwin, 1984; Valzelli, 1981). Moreover, many prepubescent children are quite aggressive before there is any significantly higher level of testosterone activity. It is a well-known fact that many women become irritable and aggressive during premenstrual periods.

There seems however, a partial, low-level correlation between the level of testosterone and aggressive behavior, especially in male adolescents and young men 17–28 years old. Moreover, XYY-genotype males who have no high level of testosterone usually do not have a high incidence of aggressive behavior.

There is no evidence that aggressive behavior is limited to the male gender. Some statistics point to the fact that more than half of crimes committed by women occur at the time of premenstrual tension. Apparently, the premenstrual period that makes many women irritable and the increased tension and the inclination to acting-out are probably related to a low level of progesterone.

It might also be advisable to mention that infectious diseases contracted by a pregnant woman could contribute to future aggressive behavior of the child. Also, a difficult and prolonged labor may cause harm to the cerebral cortex of the fetus and adversely affect the child's future behavior. It is an open question to what extent prenatal and natal adversities could be counted among the factors that predispose the formation of a sociopathic personality. Most probably all types of psychopathology, including minimal brain dysfunction, are a product of interaction between genetic, prenatal, and environmental factors (Mednick et al., 1986).

BIOCHEMICAL STUDIES

There are some indications that aggressive behavior is correlated to amino metabolism (Brown & Goodwin, 1984). Also, parachlorophenylalanine seems to be a contributing factor to antisocial behavior. A decrease in serotonin caused by lesions of the midbrain raphe nuclei may contribute to aggressiveness. Apparently, the level of serotonin metabolite 5-hydroxyindoleacetic acid in the cerebrospinal fluid is negatively correlated with violent behavior (Brown et al., 1979). The peptide group of neurotransmitters seem to stimulate impulse and aggressive behavior. Benzodiazepines, such as chlordiazepoxide and diazepam, stimulate antisocial violent behavior, and psychostimulants, such as amphetamines, are among the factors that contribute to aggressiveness. It is still an open question as whether all or how many sociopaths are motivated by any one of the above-mentioned biochemical elements.

As mentioned above, one must draw a distinction between sociopathy and other clinical types of antisocial behavior, such as encephalitis lethargica, brain tumors, psychomotor epilepsy, and head injuries (Fields & Sweet, 1975; Mark & Erwin, 1970; Monroe, 1978). Von Economo encephalitis is usually associated with hyperactivity, defects in motor coordination, and outbursts of violence. Also, schizophrenia and manic-depressive psychosis can lead to violent behavior. Paranoid schizophrenics are notoriously hostile, and other types of schizophrenics frequently experience outbursts of rage. Manic-depressive patients oscillate between self-directed and other-directed hostile feelings and at the peak of excitement may attack themselves and others.

Apparently, hostile behavior is not limited to sociopathic individuals; consider, for example, prefrontal lesions and various forms of epilepsy (Pincus, 1981).

PREFRONTAL LESIONS

Prefrontal lesions cause diverse symptoms, all of them indicative of a serious decline in self-control. They could be defined as an absence of superego with a total lack of self-criticism and consideration for other people, disappearance of moral principles, and regression to a neonatal narcissism. Prefrontal lesions are usually associated with impulsive behavior, poor judgment, lack of caution, inability to predict the consequences of one's behavior, and a tendency to thoughtless and brazen actions—all of which indicates a serious damage to the ego and, apparently, infantile regression to the uncontrollable id level. There is a striking similarity to extreme cases of sociopathic behavior.

However, the similarity between prefrontal lesion cases and sociopathic personality has its limitations, for a sociopath's intellectual functions are not affected. The IQ of sociopaths can range from the lowest to the highest levels. Sociopaths are capable of foresight and clever manipulations of other people. Sociopaths can plan their actions and avoid risky situations. In psychoanalytic language, sociopaths do not possess superegos and are narcissistic and amoral, but in most instances their egos are not impaired, with the exception of severely deteriorated cases.

ALCOHOLISM AND DRUG ADDICTION

Three of five individuals who violently assault others and/or commit murders have been under the influence of alcohol (Tinklenberg & Ochberg, 1981). Alcohol adversely affects thinking processes, and people under the influence of alcohol may act in a disinhibited, impulsive, and aggressive manner, closely resembling sociopathic behavior patterns.

Repeated alcohol intake leads to persistent disinhibited and aggressive behavior, but not all alcoholics are sociopaths and not all sociopaths are alcoholics. However, sociopaths exercise very little self-control, and all sociopaths I ever came across in private practice and hospital settings drank frequently and/or were drug users. One may question whether alcohol and drug abuse cause sociopathy, but sociopaths tend to become alcoholics and drug addicts and thus perpetuate and reinforce their antisocial behavior.

3

Sociocultural Determinants

Consider the differences between Freud's Viennese patients and contemporary American patients. Freud's clinical practice started in 1885 and for 30 years it was conducted in an atmosphere of a stable sociocultural environment and international peace. Freud's Vienna was more Victorian than London; Freud's patients were middle- and upper-class men and women; they were very traditional and quite prudish. The problems they reported to Dr. Freud were frequently related to sexual inhibitions and related issues. Hysteria was the most visible emotional disturbance, with a trickle of severe emotional disorders such as schizophrenia and manic-depressive psychosis.

Nothing of that kind exists in our times, least of all in the United States. Sexual inhibitions are today quite rare and many adolescents practice uninhibited sexual behavior. The contemporary American population faces a host of totally different problems. If one follows Ruth Benedict's distinction between the "Apollonian" type of civilization that favors peace, stability, and tradition and, on the other side, the "Dionysian" type of civilization that favors innovation, adventure, our times are certainly Dionysian rather than Apollonian (Cazeneuve, 1958).

Insecurity is probably the outstanding feature of our times.

With the exception of the super-rich, hardly anyone today is economically secure. Inflation and deflation, upsurge and downfall of national productivity, employment and unemployment, and the gyrations of securities and stock markets offer very little, if any, economic security. Hardly anyone can be in control of one's own economic future, and many people are victimized by the radical changes in economy that affect their trade or profession and can easily turn riches into rags.

Many people react to insecurity by developing feelings of depression. Depression is a feeling of helpless anger directed to oneself and to the entire world. Depressed people ask themselves, "Why am I so weak? Why can't I control my destiny? What's wrong with me?"

The other, probably less frequent reaction is the no-more-secure sociopathic attitude "No one cares for Me! No one gives a damn! Why should I care for anyone? Why not do everything for myself at the expense of other people?" The less secure one feels, the more one is inclined to distrust and suspect others. Paranoid attitudes are typical for sociopathy and are spreading like wild weeds.

THE MORAL CRISIS

Our times represent a strange combination of scientific progress on one side and of shallow hedonism, drug addictions, pseudoreligious cults and terrorism and other forms of violence on the other. Armed with the latest technological inventions, human beings can communicate over hundreds of thousands of miles, reach the moon, and fly with supersonic speed into outer space. It seems that this superhuman progress has encompassed all areas of the universe with the exclusion of human nature and human moral behavior. Driven by insecurity, contemporary human beings practice several escape devices and seek consolation in drugs, alcohol, and dishonest cults. "Having fun" seems to have become the guiding principle of our times, and the feelings of responsibility and commitment seem to lose their impact. Many people seem to believe that unfair and unethical individuals represent power and fair-minded, moral individuals are idealistic weaklings.

Selfish and reckless behavior is quite frequent in our society and it is a serious indicator of sociopathic epidemic. Lack of consideration for fellow men and inconsiderate selfishness jeopardize social bonds and may turn human society into a jungle of violence as our streets and subways offer no security.

A social scientist (Rugg, 1947) noticed that our norms are full of contradictions:

> The family is our basic institution and the sacred core of our national life. *But: Business is our most important institution . . . and other institutions must conform to its needs.*
> Honesty is the best policy. *But: Business is business and a businessman would be a fool if he didn't cover his hand.*
> Education is a fine thing. *But: It is the practical men who get things done.*
> Science is a fine thing in its place and our future depends upon it. *But: Science has no right to interfere with such things as business and our other fundamental institutions.*

Excessive selfishness, corruption, and deceit are not limited to criminals. It seems that a great many individuals have developed sociopathic traits, and the spread of sociopathy today represents a threat to the existing social order.

The decline of moral standards and the spread of dishonesty have reached the highest strata of our public life. Suffice to mention the lies of President Nixon, the shady dealings of Vice President Agnew, and the fantastic prices the Pentagon paid for coffeepots, ashtrays, and screwdrivers.

RELIGION

One may question the contribution of religion to moral behavior, for many wars and a great many acts of injustice and persecution are related to religious proselytism and fanaticism. However, a decline of religious influence has never contributed to an improvement of moral standards. Quite often noble religious devices such as "love thy neighbor" are preached but not practiced, but the loss of religious beliefs did not make the situation any better. The impact of moral teachings of religion is obviously quite limited, but a growing abandonment of places of worship deprives many people of the opportunity to listen to the voice of conscience and to develop the feeling of belonging.

On the other hand, the growth of fanatical fundamentalists and their xenophobic attitudes spreads dissent and hatred. The mushrooming of self-righteous cults fosters an atmosphere of license and lack of concern for fellow men and women, typical of sociopathic individuals.

HOSTILE BEHAVIOR

Hostile behavior is one of the main ways to cover up one's feelings of inferiority. The stronger one is, the less one needs to show one's power. Violence is the choice outlet for insecure individuals, for the amount of power needed for destructive acts is obviously much smaller than that necessary for constructive work. Scores of architects and workers spend years of effort in erecting monumental buildings, but a bomb thrown by a half-wit can instantly demolish any one of them.

The fact that one needs preciously little power for destructive action makes violence attractive to immature and maladjusted individuals torn by feelings of inadequacy and inferiority.

The more one believes in one's own power, that is, the higher one's estimate of one's power, the more one is inclined to act magnanimously. Insecure people are on guard fearing true or imaginary enemies. Insecure parents tend to be punitive, for the child's disobedience represents a threat to them. Secure parents take lightly the child's temper tantrum;

being secure, they can be understanding and magnanimous and can relate to the child in a friendly and benevolent manner. The same applies to male chauvinism and to ethnic, religious, and any other prejudice. Self-confident and self-respecting individuals do not need to put anyone down. Prejudiced individuals and racists usually suffer from a profound feeling of inferiority, and they seek self-aggrandizement by discriminating against those who cannot defend themselves.

THE SPREAD OF SOCIOPATHY

One must not overlook the contemporary mass occurrence of antisocial behavior, but one cannot assume that all terrorists and all of Hitler's followers were sociopaths. Millions of Germans who followed Hitler and committed crimes against humanity could hardly be classified as clinical sociopaths; perhaps they could be classified as "borderline sociopaths." Does this augur an era of a sort of epidemic sociopathy? Apparently, a thin line is dividing the so-called civilized behavior from sociopathy.

Evidently it is quite easy to incite people to act violently. The lynch cases of Blacks, the persecution of Jews, the slaughters of Armenians, and recent terrorism are a sad reminder of the nature of human nature. Human beings have the innate capability for love and for hate, for helping and for hurting. Human life starts in a state of total parasitism; a not-yet-born child and a newborn are takers, and they must be that way or they will not survive. It takes a good deal of growth and learning before one becomes capable of sharing and giving. Ultimately, society is based on give and take, on sharing and accommodating, and excessive selfishness jeopardizes its very existence. The mushrooming of sociopathy in our times is produced by several factors, and our sociocultural system is probably a leading factor. The present-day society is facing a vicious cycle; the decline of moral commitments fosters sociopathy, and the spreading of sociopathy further undermines moral standards.

Sociopathy seems to be *more a social than a medical problem.* There is no evidence that the tendency for violent behavior is inherited. All human beings are born with a potential for love and hate, but parents who give no love and a society that does not have clearly established moral standards backed up by a morally consistent public opinion, a society that fails to exercise to the fullest extent its obligation to protect peaceful citizens, such a society invites crime. When public opinion does not condemn unfair and unethical practices but condones them and is permissive toward dishonesty, when movies, television, and other mass media wittingly or unwittingly glorify "the tough guy" (even when he is ultimately intercepted by police, his courage and shrewdness attract unstable youngsters), when the protective and penalizing forces of society do not offer an adequate warning that could prevent sociopathic acting-out, and when public opinion does not take a clear and uncompromising stand on moral issues, the number of sociopathic individuals must be on the rise and the march of violence might continue unabated.

4

Parent-Child Interaction

THE PARENTS

Some scientists believe that sociopathy is a product of a low-socioeconomic status, and poor people who live in substandard conditions in slum areas breed antisocial children. Whereas it is a fact that these factors combined with intrafamilial dissent and violence can contribute to the development of sociopathic personalities, it must be emphasized that this is not a general rule, and there are a great many other factors that contribute to sociopathy in middle- and upper-class offspring. Family structure and intraparental and parent-child interaction are probably very important factors in the etiology of sociopathic personality (Glueck & Glueck, 1962; Krauss & Krauss, 1977; Sadoff, 1978; Wolman, 1983).

Parental socioeconomic status may play a certain role in the etiology of sociopathic personality. Levy (1951) introduced the distinction between "deprived" sociopaths who grew up in poverty and "indulged" sociopaths from upper-middle-class and wealthy homes. Wolman (1973) observed that sociopaths are often brought up in a poverty-stricken home, where parents are unable or unwilling to take care of their children, and also by wealthy parents who give their children plenty of money but no affection. Alcoholic and/or sociopathic parents, and especially fathers, play an important role in sociopathy of the offspring, but alcoholic and sociopathic fathers are not a socioeconomic phenomenon, and many middle- and upper-class families have sociopathic children.

The father of my patient, a young female sociopath, was a police officer who did not drink heavily, but treated his wife and daughter as if they were slaves. Verbal and physical abuse were common occurrences, and when the daughter reached the age of 12, he raped her frequently and forced her to have oral intercourse. Since his wife worked long hours, he managed to pick up his daughter after school and had frequent sexual relations with her. The girl did not dare tell her mother, and only three years later, when the girl got pregnant and the mother had to take her for an abortion, did the mother realize what had been going on for years.

Moreover, disturbed, sociopathic, and alcoholic parents present themselves as negative role-models to their children. They often convey the message "Do as I say, but not as I do," and the children of abusive parents follow the pattern of their antisocial parents. Quite often children of criminal fathers identify with their fathers and follow in their footsteps.

Sociopaths do not necessarily have sociopathic parents. Schizophrenic and depressed mothers tend to be inconsistent in offering guidance and setting limits, and often breed sociopathy. Parental brutality, harsh discipline or total lack of discipline, lack of economic stability, lack of guidance, and a disorganized, chaotic family life that offers no guidances, no role-models, and no sense of direction may breed exceedingly selfish, exploitative, sociopathic children with a "sink-or-swim" mentality.

Lack of parental love and emotional deprivation most often lead to a sense of loneliness and desire to get even with whoever does not comply with whims and wishes of the rejected child. However, not all rejected children become sociopaths, and one need not exclude the possibility of genetic predisposition.

LACK OF AFFECTION

Several studies point to a peculiar lack of warmth between the parents and the child who becomes a sociopath. The children grow up as if they were orphans forced from the earliest years to take care of themselves and fight for survival. The sociopathic child fails to develop any conception of right and wrong and, consequently, is incapable of experiencing moral guilt feelings. From the earliest years the sociopathic child had to rely on oneself without being able to rely on human friendship, sympathy, and affection. This sink-or-swim mentality results in perceiving the world as a hostile place where justice, mercy, consideration, and compassion are nonexistent, and where one can survive only at the expense of others.

Adult sociopaths do not have stable and affectionate human relationships. Their life histories, even when they were brought up in wealthy families, resemble the lives of wayward children. No one has ever cared for them and no one has ever loved them. They experience continuous emotional neglect and develop no attachment to anyone because there was no one trustworthy, stable, and reliable to depend on. In some cases the mother was severely disturbed and unable to care for the presociopathic child; in other cases she didn't care to take care of the child and left the child with relatives, nurses, or on the street. No sociopath is proud of his or her parents, nor do they experience tender feelings toward their parents. This applies to children of slums and of wealthy suburban families alike; in slums no one could care for the child; in wealthy homes no one would. Bandura and Walters (1959), O'Neal et al. (1962), and others found that sociopathic personality in children is highly related to parental desertion, lack of support, and emotional deprivation.

A study of juvenile delinquency and disturbances in acculturation found sociopathic features closely related to decline in parental authority and to loosening of family bonds caused by migration and acculturation (Wolman, 1949).

LACK OF GUIDANCE

Some sociopaths come from families rich in money and poor in love who do not teach the child moral values nor do they foster inhibition of impulses. The sociopaths learn to get whatever they want without consideration for others. Vacillating, morally weak, hyperpermissive, and not-caring parents foster selfish, sociopathic personality development. A description of a young sociopathic patient may elucidate the point:

Why did he take LSD? The 19-year-old man sat stiffly on the chair in my office. He had just admitted that he had been taking the hallucinatory drug, and before that he had taken "pot." And now he was in a state of panic. He was petrified; he felt he was losing his mind.

"Doc," he whispered, "what else can one do? What is this all about?"

He trembled. He was both scared and bewildered. He came to me asking for help. He wanted to get rid of the unbearable tension and the terror.

He was a bright young man, a student in a private university. His father was a real-estate broker, his mother was a socialite, and his older sister was married to a business executive. They lived in a mansion in a fashionable community on Long Island. They owned three new cars and belonged to a country club. The father was a board member of a charity organization and the mother was a president of a church sorority.

The young man was one of thousands of young adults who have lost their sense of direction in life, or perhaps never had it. Were they poor, psychologists or sociologists could have called them "wayward youth." But they were members of the opulent social class.

All their physical needs were taken care of, but a life of plenty is not necessarily a happy life. People may get fed up with food, bored with bread, sick of sex, tired of travel, and disenchanted with enchantment.

Apparently, parents who give freedom to the child's impulses prevent growth or foster regression. Some parents, unwilling or unable to control their children, let them grow in savagery, permitting "free" sex and violence.

INFERIORITY FEELING

As a result of deep inferiority feelings combined with a lack of love for anyone, some sociopaths act aggressively in order to demonstrate their power. Sociopaths are prone to torture and mutilate in robbery and rape, because an exercise of cruelty enhances their feeling of power. Many sociopaths attack, torture, and murder, displaying inhuman cruelty and deriving pleasure from these actions.

Most lower-class children live in a homogeneous lower-class neighborhood and attend public school in which all other children have the same or a similar background. In many instances the teachers come from the middle class, or in their college education they have acquired middle-class manners. Most often the language the teachers use differs considerably from the language the low-class child hears at home. The school situation presents the lower-class children with considerable adjustment problems, and some children develop feelings of inferiority that adversely affect their academic performance. Some children develop a negative and even hostile attitude to the teachers and the middle-class values the teachers represent. Antisocial behavior is, to some extent, related to overassertion as a reaction to inferiority feelings.

ISOLATION

Several years ago at a third or fourth psychotherapeutic session a 22-year-old sociopath turned to me, apparently embarrassed, and told me that he is not able to come to me. "You see, Dr. Wolman, everybody says that you are an excellent shrink, but you are Jewish, and I cannot relate to you. It will not work." "OK," I replied, "I am teaching in a medical school and there are many non-Jewish psychiatrists and psychologists. Dr. A. is a Protestant and a superb clinician. Would you like me to refer you to Dr. A.?" "Oh, no," my patient said, "the Protestants are worse than the Jews!" "I did not know that," I remarked, "but would you prefer Dr. B., who is an excellent doctor and a Catholic?" "Catholics!" my patient exclaimed, "They are the worst of all!"

He told me the following story. His parents were Hungarian Catholics who migrated to the United States many years ago. He himself was born in New York. His father somehow adjusted to the new environment, but his mother disliked everyone, avoided social contacts, and was often depressed. At the age of six the patient went to a public school in Brooklyn and got friendly with several classmates.

Once he brought home a black child. His father was friendly to little Steve, but his mother was livid.

"Aren't you ashamed to bring that 'nigger' home?" she shouted. My patient tried to defend his friend: "Ma, he is such a nice kid, he plays with me, he always helps me." The mother sent the black child away. A week later the boy brought another friend home. They played together and the mother seemed to be pleased. When the little boy left, the mother asked the name of the boy. His name was Goldstein. "He must be Jewish!" the mother exclaimed. "I don't allow you to play with people who killed Christ!"

The next day my patient interrogated his Jewish friend. The little Goldstein denied having killed anybody, but my patient's mother was adamant and forced him to break off with his Jewish friend. A few weeks later he was invited by another boy, Jim McMahon. This time he thoroughly investigated his friend. The friend was white and Christian, he didn't kill anyone, and was going to Church with his parents. My patient triumphantly reported to the mother his visit with the McMahons. But, to his mother's great dismay, Jim McMahon happened to be a Protestant and "Protestants, as everyone knows, are not good Christians," the mother emphasized.

My patient felt more and more restricted in the choice of friends. When he finally made friends with Catholic children, they too were rejected by his mother. It was not good enough to be a Catholic if your name was Napolitano, for "everyone should know that Italians are criminals and belong to the Mafia." A year later my patient got friendly with and brought home Charlie O'Leary, but the mother maintained that the Irish are not good Catholics because they are drunkards. My patient, who was eight years old, visited the O'Leary family and discovered that they were not alcoholics and drank less than his parents, but it did not help.

Years later he discovered a *"landsman"*—a boy born in Hungary, but the mother hated Hungarians. In his teens he tried to associate with his cousins, but his mother was not on speaking terms with her family. "My two sisters and their husbands are a bunch of crooks and I do not allow you to have anything to do with them," she said.

And so my patient lived in almost total isolation, full of paranoid fear and hatred of the entire world, convinced that the whole world was about "to get him," that his father was against him, and the mother was one of his enemies.

REJECTION AND ANTISOCIAL BEHAVIOR

Rejected and emotionally starved children often resort to aggressiveness as compensatory mechanisms. The first few years of a child's life are the most important in terms of psychological development. During these years, depending on the attitudes of individuals in his close environment, he or she develops a feeling of security or insecurity. Either serves as a basis for personality development.

Many mothers do not want the children that they have.

These children are often rejected and treated with abuse and neglect (Berkowitz, 1962). This reinforces the child's feeling of insecurity and undermines his conception of oneself as a person of value and significance. Sometimes the child feels that parental aggression is justified because he or she feels worthless. The child may have a fear of being destroyed because he or she feels like a weak, unprotected individual owing to his parents' lack of concern. He or she distrusts and resents others because there is no reason to trust or like anyone. A prolonged and severe rejection produces in the child feelings of defiance and mistrust that can verge on the paranoid and lead to an overall sense of hostility for self-defense. In order to protect oneself and overcome the feeling of inadequacy, the child may resort to aggression. If he is strong enough and by aggressive means can assert himself and receive a feeling of power, he will continue the aggressive behavior. Hoffman, Rosen, and Lippitt (1960) found that children who felt that they were alone and who lacked a sense of power as compared to the authority of their parents acted aggressively in order to express themselves. This method of assertion was generalized to their peer group. Rejection by one's parents may teach the child that all other humans are hostile and aggressive and antisocial behavior must extend to all situations.

LACK OF ATTENTION

For young children attention is a sign of love and interest. When a child is not able to obtain attention in his home, he may resort to aggression. Apparently, there is a positive relationship between inadequate attention in the home and aggressive behavior. Children brought up in homes where little attention is given to them tend to display a higher level of aggression.

The sociopath has a distorted and bleak conception of the world. His perception is one of emptiness followed by the perception of grabbing, fighting, fusing, or eating up parts of the environment. The sociopath perceives any close contact with his mother as a potential threat because he has been repudiated and thwarted so inconsistently by an unstable and/or absent mother. The child turns to antisocial behavior as a means of handling his loss of parents and as a means of receiving the gratification his parents fail to give.

An inadequate parent-child relationship contributes to sociopathic personality. Research suggests that the sociopathic child fails to accept social controls because of parental ineffectiveness at socialization of their child (Barron, 1954, p. 131). Parents are often rejecting and affectionless toward this child. "Inasmuch as his parents typify the community to the child, he is likely to become an aggressive, rebellious, hostile, and hyperactive person who engages in delinquent activities" (Barron, 1954, p. 132).

MATERNAL DEPRIVATION

Every child requires an affectionate relationship with his mother. If a warm relationship is not established, anxiety feelings result in a state of "maternal deprivation." Severe deprivation results in keen anxiety and an inordinate need for love and strong feelings of revenge.

Maternal rejection and emotional instability frequently appear in the case histories of delinquents. Wilson's study of "problem families" in Cardiff, England, has revealed maternal deprivation in every home that produced a juvenile delinquent (Wilson, 1958). When the mother is absent, neglectful, ambivalent, or insecure, the child fails to receive some stable "source of satisfaction." The child is continually disappointed when care is "insufficient or impersonal" and he refrains from transforming his narcissistic energy into an object external to himself. The child withdraws his love from the object-world and places stronger emphasis on his narcissistic and autoerotic pleasure. The future sociopath tends toward "rocking, sucking, and masturbation." The child's libido remains self-cathected, and the destructive forces fail to be adequately harnessed. The destructive energies "remain more isolated and manifest themselves more independently in various ways from merely overemphasized aggressiveness to wanton destructiveness" (Freud, 1949, p. 194) that is typical for sociopaths.

Normally the young child displays destructive and disorderly behavior when his encounters with the environment prove to be upsetting. Children act in accordance with what they perceive, not in accordance with reality. When the mother does not meet the child's needs, the child does not develop a trust and security in her as one who satisfies his needs. If the child fails to receive love and affection, the oral-sadistic impulses become directed toward the mother and sociopathic children often develop hatred for their mothers. When they perceive her as one who rejects and hates, the hate toward the mother may expand toward the external world.

The child's ambivalent image of his mother as one who cares and as someone who is hostile increases the child's hostile feelings. The child attempts to deny his feelings toward the mother and the feelings of her hatred. Many a sociopath uses projection to defend oneself from the self-consuming rage and despair, but the hatred usually extends to include the entire world. The lack of love, replaced by intense hatred, prevents the sociopathic child from developing a superego-conscience necessary for adequate social interactions.

This hostile and rejecting attitude toward the parents fosters sociopathy. The child fails to identify with the parents and thereby fails to internalize their values and a superego. Behavior that might displease the parent is not inhibited, but may instead yield gratification and pleasure, and the parental image is no longer an acceptable model for conformity.

Rewards and attention are usually received from imitation of an adult model. As a result of imitating his parents, the child learns to "reward himself by expression of self-approval and self-love" (Bandura & Walters, 1959, pp. 54–55). Parental attitudes and values are learned on the cognitive and covert levels. The aggressive sociopathic child fails to internalize parental values and is devoid of internal controls (Bandura & Walters, 1959, p. 62). He continues to feel fear, abhorrence, and dislike toward the parents who take no interest or act cruelly to him, and his moral development is blunted (Wolfe, 1949, p. 266).

Bandura and Walters (1959) studied 52 adolescent boys, aged 14 and 17 years, and their parents. Twenty-six of the boys showed "aggressive and destructive" behavior, and 26 boys had been evaluated as both nonaggressive and noninhibited. The subjects were whites, from middle-class homes in a neighborhood that was not deteriorated or a juvenile or adult delinquency area. The parents were steadily employed, and their intelligence was average or above average.

Comparison with nonaggressive adolescents has shown that the parents of antisocial boys have shown less affection and were more rejecting than the parents of nondelinquent boys. Delinquent boys felt rejected by their parents (Andry, 1962; Bandura & Walters, 1959).

Apparently, a child's ego is strengthened each time the child endures frustrations, denies his instinctual drives, and controls overt behavior. When the parents provide love, stability, and trust for the child, they contribute to the child's wholesome development. The disturbance in the ego development occurs in cases of long separations from the mother before age three, as well as when the unstable personality of the mother makes her act inconsistently "during feeding, weaning and toilet training" (Friedlander, 1949, p. 206).

LATENCY PERIOD

At the age 6 to 11 or 12, children tend to develop strong bonds to their parents and especially to the parent of the same gender. They are moving in the direction of psychosexual identification, and they become quite dependent on parental guidance, control, and approval. The boy's dependency needs can be severely frustrated by parental rejection and lack of love (Bandura & Walters, 1959) when the father is indifferent and fails to give attention, love, and guidance.

Lacking love and unable to develop internalized controls, a child is thrust into social isolation during the latency period. The child has great difficulty in accepting school authority and falls behind in his schoolwork. The sociopathic child defies the school by becoming a truant or disobeys the teachers and rebels against school rules and regulations.

During the latency period the sociopath's psychosexual identification remains on a rather immature level. The superego does not function, and consequently no guilt feelings are produced; the child continues to act as if he or she were an impulsive infant and unable to break away from the "pleasure principle." The acting-out sociopathic child needs continuous external control in order to comply with school discipline (Friedlander, 1949). As contact with people broadens, during the latency period, the sociopathic child fails to differentiate between emotionally important and emotionally insignificant people, emotionally supportive and nonsupportive people. The paranoid tendency grows as the child begins to view all people either as those who succumb to his wishes or as potential enemies.

ADOLESCENCE

By the time the sociopathic child reaches adolescence, there is a complete breakdown in any internal control. The absence of self-control and of a superego in the sociopathic adolescent's behavior is called "superego lacunea" (Johnson, 1959, p. 225). An adequate superego can be formed when the child is given constructive guidance by a stable parent who gives orders and expects them to be carried out.

During adolescence the hostility and aggression that have

been building up through the developmental phases break through. A delinquent often describes his parents as devoid of affection toward him and as overly authoritarian (Berman, 1959, pp. 613–614). Instead of love he has experienced "frustration, distrust and a most intense hate" (Berman, 1959, p. 620).

PARENTAL VIOLENCE

Parker and Allerton (1962) quoted a criminal who described violence in his childhood as follows: "As long as I can remember I have seen violence in use all around me— my mother hitting the children, my brothers and sisters all whacking their mother or other children, the man downstairs bashing his wife and so on."

A young sociopathic woman described her childhood as follows: "My parents hated each other and often engaged in verbal and physical fights. There was never a shortage of money in our house, but both begrudged me when I asked for money. When I was 16 and had my first date, I borrowed my mother's high-heel shoes. When I came home late in the evening, my mother waited for me and with a broomstick in her hand. She split my skull, and I was taken by an ambulance to an emergency room in a hospital."

Some parents of sociopaths openly and actively practice hostile and violent behavior. According to Bandura et al. (1961), parental attacks on a child, verbal or physical, and a continuous hostile attitude, criticisms, and threat of violence strongly contribute to the formation of antisocial and violent behavior in the child.

PART II

Symptomatology

5

The Narcissistic-Parasitic Personality

"THE REFUGEE"

He came to my office with a smile on his face. He knew very well what it was all about. He had already seen several psychiatrists and psychologists, and some of them had been kind enough and put in writing that he needed help.

He was unemployed, 40 years old, single, and had no permanent address. He introduced himself as "a mental case," and as such he did not need "any of these things." For the last few years he has been busy collecting money necessary for his "treatment." He was in trouble with the post office for his illegal use of mail for collections, but besides that things were going well and, he assured me, he was never late in paying doctor's fees.

How? Very simple. He was a refugee, he said, for over 20 years, and he is still a refugee. He knocks at the doors of his more fortunate friends who came with him together to this country about 20 years ago. All of them got jobs, were married, and had children. They were refugees in the past, but they are no longer refugees. He, the poor soul, could not help himself because he is a "mental case." Social agencies misunderstood the severity of his problems and instead of just paying him a weekly subsistence, insisted that he should get a job and go to work. But, of course, they failed, for he refused to go to work. Work is hard; it is hot in the summer, cold in the winter, there is rain in the mornings, winds in the evenings, and subways are crowded. How can a person with mental problems hold a job? No, this was too much for him.

He told me that he embarked on a new idea. He goes to the house of one of those fortunate ex-refugees who knew him from childhood. There he starts a hunger strike until the friend agrees to give him money, and he collects a couple of hundred dollars. No friend would let him starve himself to death and die in his house!

He goes from one friend to another and repeats the same show.

Then he looks for "treatment." He asks the kind doctors to state in writing how badly he needs psychotherapy. When his money reserves reach a low level, he discontinues treatment and he uses the doctors' statements to get more money. Whenever his money is "short," he settles down in a friend's house and threatens the friend with another hunger strike. In between he travels to Florida and takes summer and winter vacations in various resorts; of course, all this in order to alleviate his terrible mental condition that could be incurable and requires lifelong treatment.

INNOCENT CRIMINALS

Another man referred to me by his family had been forging checks. He never forged checks of his friends or family, he said. New York City, he said, was wasting so much public money that he felt entitled to take some of the city's money. He assured me that he did not need any therapy, but his stupid old parents forced him to come to my office. He promised not to forge my checks or bills; he was never unfair to "nice people."

Another man was referred to my office by his family physician. His wife annoyed him. He was unemployed and untrained and needed money for business. He married the daughter of a wealthy man who put him in business. The business was doing very well; there are many foolish people to whom one can sell old stuff as if it were new. In his free time he likes to go out with "girls." What does his wife want from him? He "made" her a baby to keep her busy. When the infant was born, his wife and her family insisted that he spend some time at home. Presently, he developed short breath, perspiration, and a heart condition, and all of these symptoms occur only at home. He gets dizzy whenever his wife asks him to change diapers. He went to a family physician, was thoroughly examined, and referred for psychotherapy. The family doctor told me the man was in perfect physical condition.

Of course, he did not believe his doctor; the doctor did not do a good job. Probably the doctor was bribed by his wife's family.

A 24-year-old woman came to my office asking for help. She was exceedingly polite and spoke in a sugar-sweet voice. She had, so she said, some undescribable physical condition: she was often out of breath and in hot weather perspired profusely. She went to three doctors and none of them could diagnose her, so she "forced her parents" to pay for her psychotherapy. She was the only child and her "mean parents" could not care about her and expected her to go to work.

Two sociopathic women told me how they physically assaulted their mothers. Basically, they said, they were friendly to their mothers, but sometimes "people must be put in their place." Anyway, they did not hit very hard.

Several years ago I taught in a postdoctoral program in psychiatry and supervised a few residents. Once the resident I supervised was called to the emergency room and I went with him. Two policemen brought in a young man who murdered or tried to murder his estranged wife. The young man greeted both of us politely and cheerfully and told us the following story: He had a wife and a baby, but she was "very selfish and demanding" and he "got rid of her." The wife and the child moved to his in-laws. And this is what had happened just today. He didn't feel well and decided to stay home; at noon he went to a neighborhood restaurant for lunch. When he came back, he found his estranged wife "snooping" in *his* home at *his* desk! "I am looking for the child's birth certificate," she said. "What right do you have to come to *my* home? Give me back the keys to my home! I will teach you a lesson!" he told her. He went to the kitchen, picked up the heaviest hammer, and "topped" her on the head.

The young man turned to the resident and asked: "Doctor, wouldn't you do the same? What right does she have to snoop around? When she fell on the floor, bleeding, I called for an ambulance! Don't you think," he asked, "I was right? Wasn't I kind to that bitch?"

PARASITIC ATTITUDES

One must draw a distinction between violent and nonviolent sociopaths. All of them are exceedingly selfish, overdemanding, manipulative, and exploitative. None of them has anything resembling a superego or any remorse or guilt feelings. All of them are prone to lie, cheat, take advantage, exploit, and are always ready to justify their dishonest behavior. All of them are sensitive to pain and tend to be hypochondriacs. They never blame themselves but tend to be hostile and harbor paranoid suspicions and accusations. They believe themselves to be "innocent victims" of adverse conditions and/or hostile environments and justify their hostile attitudes by the need to defend themselves.

In most situations, sociopaths try to win attention and approval and present themselves as victims of "unfair treatment" and of "lack of luck." They tend to be totally *parasitic*, as if regressing to earliest days of infancy and expecting the entire world to act as a milk-giving mother. A 32-year-old man, who was admitted in an executive capacity to his in-laws' flourishing business, was coming to the office in the morning for two or three hours and stealing whatever cash he could. He usually lunched with one of his girlfriends and spent the afternoons in a luxurious apartment he purchased with the money stolen from his in-laws' business. After all, he said, he was a young man and had the right to enjoy himself.

Every sociopath is selfish and manipulative. They care only for themselves and use others as tools for their own satisfaction. I called them "narcissistic hyper-instrumentals" (Wolman, 1973). Shapiro (1965) calls them "impulsive psychopathic characters." They are bent on immediate gratification of their needs and exercise very little, if any, self-criticism. They are always self-centered and preoccupied with sensuous pleasures and, therefore, are prone to sexual promiscuity and perversion and alcohol and drug abuse. They get angry when confronted with a difficult task and always demand special privileges no one else receives. They tend to be negligent and dishonest on their jobs. They get angry when their superiors present them with a job that requires effort. They perceive demands as an imposition and try to evade difficulty by cheating or rebellion, depending on the estimate of the adversary's strength.

HYPOCHONDRIASIS

Let us proceed from the general description of the sociopathic personality to specific symptoms.

Being exceedingly selfish and overconcerned with their own self-being, sociopaths tend to worry about their health and appearance. They tend to seek medical help whenever there is the tiniest or even a nonexisting threat to their health. A mild cold, a tiny blemish, indigestion, or a slight feeling of discomfort drives them to the doctor's office. All sociopathic patients I have seen in 40 years of my clinical practice were hypochondriacs, and most of them were referred to my office by physicians who could not discover any physical ailment, and told the complaining sociopaths that the problem must be psychological. Then, the sociopaths sought psychological help.

SEXUAL BEHAVIOR

Eros, the drive of love, and Ares, the hostile drive, are never completely separated in sociopathic individuals. In sociopaths Eros is subservient to Ares and sex is often combined with violence. Many sociopaths are and remain lifelong "polymorphous perverts," who practice masturbation, homosexuality, fellatio, and pedophilia. Some of them practice sexual relations with infants, senile women, and anyone available when they are sexually aroused. The "pleasure principle," that is, the principle of immediate gratification of needs, is the main motive in the life of sociopaths.

LYING

One must draw a distinction between perceptual distortions and memory lapses on one side and sociopathic lying. Perceptual distortions are frequent occurrences in childhood, and memory defects may occur at any age to any individual. Observational statements or reports may not agree with reality for a variety of reasons, but they are not lies as long as they are not intentional.

Lies are intentionally misleading verbal and nonverbal communications. Many people lie occasionally, but sociopaths lie on every possible occasion and feel no regrets, no remorse, and no guilt. Adult sociopaths do not confabulate like little children nor do they suffer memory losses like Alzheimer victims. They lie all the time, consciously and intentionally, and their lies help them to take advantage of other people. Sociopaths are deliberate liars who use lying for deceiving, cheating, and outsmarting, always for their own material or any other gain.

Sociopaths tend to project their thoughts and feelings.

Some of my sociopathic patients were convinced that everybody else was a liar. They could not believe that other people told the truth and felt guilty whenever they told a lie. My sociopathic patients were sure that people who denied lying were the greatest liars.

ALCOHOLISM

Not all alcoholics are sociopaths and not all sociopaths are alcoholics, but there is a definite and a high correlation between sociopathy and alcoholism. The first *Diagnostic and Statistical Manual* of the American Psychiatric Association (published in 1952) listed alcoholism under the category of sociopathic disorder. The third edition of the *Manual* (DSM-III), published in 1980, listed alcoholism as a separate category, not included in the disorder of antisocial personality. Obviously, alcoholic addiction is a widespread phenomenon not limited to sociopathy.

Moreover, one must draw a distinction between alcoholism as a continuous pattern of behavior and the antisocial behavior of an intoxicated individual. A temporary state of alcoholic intoxication of a nonalcoholic may lead to violent behavior, but sociopaths do not need alcohol as motivation for crime. In most instances they tend to act out when they are sober; most often their selfish, antisocial actions are calculated, carefully planned, and aimed at some sort of gain. They rarely, if ever, attack powerful adversaries; usually they go for a sure victory, whether it is money or sex or anything else, whereas nonsociopathic alcoholics tend to act on impulse. Most sociopathic alcoholics prefer to rape children rather than adults, for children cannot defend themselves and sociopaths prefer not to take chances. Almost all rape cases of old women are committed by sociopaths, as rape gives them a double pleasure of sex and power. Many of them drink before raping, for alcohol reduces fear and enhances their feeling of power.

The sociopath's alcohol abuse and antisocial behavior start

in early teens. Early alcoholism is often associated with other patterns of antisocial behavior, such as truancy, disobedience, and disrespect for teachers, extorting money from schoolmates, occasional violence, running away from home, and joining criminal gangs. Heavy beer drinking is a frequent phenomenon. Quite often sociopathic alcoholics gang up on a lonely girl and rape her, taking turns one after another (Rada, 1978). One of my female patients was raped by a gang of her classmates when she was a high-school sophomore; all of them were heavy drinkers.

As the sociopathic alcoholic grows up, he becomes more abusive toward peers and parents. Sociopaths always maintain that their victims "provoked" them and "started the fight." One college boy told me that he could have "broken his father's arm," but, of course, "he was very considerate." When his father accused him of being a "bum and an alcoholic," he merely "hit his father once and threw him on the floor," and "his father deserved a more severe punishment."

DRUG DEPENDENCE

Drug dependence or drug abuse is not a clinical entity, despite the DSM-III. Drug dependence is a widespread behavioral pattern that can be associated with a variety of mental disorders as well as with some otherwise normal personalities. Many manic-depressive and schizophrenic patients are drug addicts, and some normal individuals may become addicted, when due to a physical illness they had to take addictive painkillers or some other habit-forming medications.

Drug dependence or addiction or abuse (I am using all these terms interchangeably) is not limited to sociopaths nor are all sociopaths drug addicts. However, many sociopaths are drug users and many drug users are sociopaths. All sociopaths are notorious pleasure-seeking and pain-avoiding individuals and exercise poor, if any, self-control; as such,

The Narcissistic-Parasitic Personality

they are prone to turn to drugs. When they are forced to undergo institutional treatment, they tend to justify their behavior and to blame everyone else for their addiction, as they believe they are victims of unfavorable circumstances and/or unfair people.

AGING

As sociopaths get older, their moral standards do not change, but they become more cautious, more exploitative, and more cunning. Frequently they are in a bad mood, complaining about the unfair world and the true or imaginary injustices they have suffered. In old age they become even more bitter, grouchy, and hypochondriac, full of hatred toward their "mean" spouses and "ungrateful" children. They tend to feel "burnt out" and disgusted with life and complain to their friends and relatives that they have "nothing to live for." They say that they plan to commit suicide, but they never do it. I did come across two cases of fake suicide, when two old sociopathic women emptied bottles of sleeping pills and phoned their relatives pretending that they were just about to die. Their suicidal threats were aimed at eliciting guilt feelings in their relatives and extorting attention, compassion, and care.

Many old sociopaths, men and women alike, tend to become more and more cynical and hostile. They ascribe hatred and antisocial behavior to the entire world. They do not believe that anyone is fair minded, and they maintain that the world is full of liars, crooks, and criminals, and that their own actions are a necessary case of self-defense. However, their acting-out and verbal and physical abusive behavior is gradually reduced.

DSM-III

Let us conclude the chapter by quotes from the *DSM-III* (1980, pp. 317–319).

301.70. Antisocial Personality Disorder

The essential feature is a Personality Disorder in which there are a history of continuous and chronic antisocial behavior in which the rights of others are violated, persistence into adult life of a pattern of antisocial behavior that began before the age of 15, and failure to sustain good job performance over a period of several years. . . .

Lying, stealing, fighting, truancy, and resisting authority are typical early childhood signs. In adolescence, unusually early or aggressive sexual behavior, excessive drinking, and use of illicit drugs are frequent. In adulthood, these kinds of behavior continue, with the addition of inability to sustain consistent work performance or to function as a responsible parent and failure to accept social norms with respect to lawful behavior. After age 30 the more flagrant aspects may diminish, particularly sexual promiscuity, fighting, criminality, and vagrancy. . . .

Predisposing Factors. . . . The absence of parental discipline apparently increases the likelihood that Conduct Disorder will develop into Antisocial Personality Disorder. Other predisposing factors include extreme poverty, removal from the home, and growing up without parental figures of both sexes. . . .

Sex ratio. The disorder is much more common in males than in females.

Prevalence. Estimates of the prevalence of Antisocial Personality Disorder for American men are about 3%, and for American women, less than 1%. The disorder is more common in lower-class populations partly because it is associated with impaired earning capacity and partly because fathers of those with the disorder frequently have the disorder themselves, and consequently their children often grow up in impoverished homes.

Familial Pattern. Antisocial Personality Disorder is particularly common in the fathers of both males and females with the disorder. Studies attempting to separate genetic from environmental influences within the family suggest that both are important, since there seems to be inheritance from biological fathers separated from their offspring early in life and a social influence from adoptive fathers. Because of a tendency toward assortative mating, the children of women with Antisocial Personality Disorder who have the disorder themselves are likely to have both a mother and a father with the disorder.

6

Aggressive and Violent Behavior

VIOLENCE

Not all sociopaths are violent and not all violent individuals are sociopaths. Many adult people are capable of some degree of self-control and can restrain their urge to strike out and the restraint can be motivated by fear of consequences (ego) or related to feelings of guilt (superego). Sociopaths crave power at any price and practice self-assertion at the expense of others, which gives them the feeling of power.

There are, however, several pathological but nonsociopathic cases of unrestrained violent behavior. Consider psychomotor epileptics who get violent without being aware of what they are doing. As mentioned in previous chapters, aggressive behavior is typical for many other clinical types such as certain types of schizophrenia and in depression.

Depression is a feeling of helpless anger directed to oneself. Depressed patients hate themselves; they wish to be loved and hate those who do not love them.

Severe depression is loaded with hostility and fraught with suicidal danger. Agitated-depressed patients feel gloomy and angry, rejected and despised, hated and hateful. One patient described his feelings: "I feel like jumping out of my skin. Doctor Wolman, please lock me up before I strangle my wife and my child. . . . I cannot stand them. I hate them and hate myself." A female depressed patient felt tortured by an unbearable state of depression and resented her adult children (she was a widow) who were "too busy" with their own activities. She hated them and herself. Her son's lack of interest in her precipitated a violent destructive and self-destructive reaction, and any sign of rejection had unleashed in her uncontrollable outbursts of violence.

Animal Violence

Violent behavior is not limited to the human race. Human beings are not the biggest or the strongest creatures, but they are certainly the most belligerent ones, second only to rats. Human beings have frequently engaged in intraspecific, intragroup, and fratricidal wars. Living together offers numerous opportunities for cooperation, as described by the anarchist philosopher Peter Kropotkin, and intraspecific cooperation increases the chances for survival of the members of the group. In many instances herbiverous animals form a defensive ring against predatory beasts. On the other hand, a pack of wolves has a better chance of killing a deer than a single wolf. However, this unity does not last long. When a herd of herbivorous animals runs over a cliff escaping from danger, stronger animals push the weaker ones down into the abyss. As soon as the hunt is over, wolves fight one another for a bigger share.

Human Violence

Human beings do the same, and they may outdo animals. As soon as the persecution of Christians in Rome came to an end, the Christians began to persecute others. The "great" French revolutionaries, who rebelled against the King's tyranny, sent to death not only enemies but also their most ardent supporters, the Hebertists. Soon the Reign of Terror

Aggressive and Violent Behavior

had its Thermidor, and Robespierre was a victim of his favorite guillotine. The victorious Russian Communists, as soon as they defeated the counterrevolutionary "white" armies, attacked the anarchists and the left-wing Social-Revolutionaries who had helped them in the October Revolution. After Lenin's death, his disciples, led by Stalin, engaged for decades in mass murder of their devoted comrades.

The Biblical myth of Cain and Abel is a case in point, and so is the story of Romulus and Remus. Territorial wars are called "patriotic"; intragroup wars are called various fancy names. In the Religious Wars of the sixteenth and seventeenth centuries, the good Christians who prayed (in Latin) to the God of mercy murdered other good Christians who prayed to the same God (in another language). During the American Civil War (1861–1865) more lives were lost than in any other war the Americans fought.

Weakness encourages aggression, and balance of power (which is a euphemistic expression of fear of retaliation) restrains it. The Roman Empire did come, temporarily, to terms with the powerful Parthians but destroyed the Jewish Temple and tortured the Christians. The Catholic Church persecuted Jews and heretics (Albigenses, Waldenses, Hussites, and others) who had never represented a real threat to the Church, but they did not declare a war against the powerful Greek Orthodox Church that dared to break away and challenged the papal authority. Roman Catholics, so eager to burn John Huss alive, did not dare to set Constantinople or Moscow afire. They incited the Polish kings, Stefan Batory and Zygmunt Waza, against the Greek Orthodox Christians but never declared a Holy War nor instituted an Inquisition against them. Wars become "holy" when one is sure of victory, and there are good chances for looting; otherwise, they are just "necessary" wars.

In the 1930s the Germans "needed" Polish wheat, French iron, and Caucasian oil; they also needed to prove their military power. Today, after having lost World War II, the Germans are economically and in any other way better off than they ever were before, even at the peak of their Hitlerite glory. The war was, as it usually is, an insane act leading to mass destruction and mass murder with no real gain for anyone. Were Germans a pack of wolves, no Hitler-type leader could have led them to do what they did, but in the human nature there is room for Nazism, mass murder, and concentration camps. Germany was "overpopulated" in 1939 and needed *Lebensraum;* after the war the Germans from Silesia and Sudeten immigrated to Germany, and there was no overpopulation at all. In the Thirty Years' War the Emperor of the Holy Roman Empire wanted to confiscate the secularized Church property, and the pious Protestant Lords joined Luther in order to grab the property that belonged to the Church. The Holy Crusades, started by the inspiring words *"C'est le Dieu qui veut"* ("God wills it"), invoked the good Lord for the benefit of merchants from Venice and the Byzantine rulers who paid well for the "holy" enterprise.

In the past one had to use a sword to kill one "enemy" at a time; the indolent and ineffectual Crusaders killed a couple hundred thousand defenseless Jews, and the total loss of human life in the Hundred Years War was less than in Vietnam. In modern times 6 million Jews and 4 million other people were gassed in a spectacularly short time, and 40 million were murdered elsewhere. In the "primitive," "barbaric" past, prior to the great advent of modern technology, world wars were unthinkable, but in our modern, highly civilized era, we have had two world wars in one century, and a most spectacular third one lurks around the corner.

As mentioned earlier, violence is not necessarily and not always associated with hatred. Julius Caesar did not hate the Gauls; he simply subjugated them. Napoleon did not hate the Spaniards; he merely wanted his family to rule the world. The Gauls hated Julius Caesar and fought against him, and the Spaniards hated Napoleon and offered a desperate resistance to his armies. Apparently the defenders hate the aggressors; do the aggressors hate their victims?

Great criminals and conquerors tend to make excuses for their aggressions. Hitler never expressed hatred for Austria and Czechoslovakia; he just "needed" to occupy them. When he attacked Poland on September 1, 1939, he ordered some of his henchmen to shoot at his own border guards. At sunrise he announced on the radio that the Poles opened fire on German soldiers *und es wird zurückgeschossen* ("the fire has been returned"). The apparent lie had a purpose: to prevent or at least to slow down allied help to Poland.

According to their virulent propaganda, the Nazis hated all Jews, but they certainly "loved" Jewish money, gold extracted from Jewish teeth, soap cakes made of Jewish bones, and lampshades made of Jewish skin. It is quite possible that the Nazis hated the Japanese more than the Jews, but the Jews have always been an easy scapegoat. The French might dislike the British and vice versa, but the chances of a war across the Channel could be substantially increased if one of the two nations were to become an easy target. The Communist rulers of Russia hated Red China more than they hated Dubcek's Czechoslovakia, but in 1968 they occupied Prague and not Peking. The Czechoslovakians raised their fists in helpless hatred and shouted: "You are Nazis! Go home!" But the Russian tanks opened fire unemotionally and imposed their iron rule over the country they did not hate at all.

Quite often outbursts of human violence resemble animal "mobbing." At the sight of an intruder birds attack the common enemy en masse, no matter who he is. The fights between Moslems and Hindus in India, Protestants and Catholics in Belfast, and the persecution of Kurds in Iran and Armenians in Turkey are not recollections from the Stone Age or from intrahuman races. They are recent and contemporary phenomena; apparently dark ages continue unabated, and as will be described later, the times seem to get even darker.

Usually human cruelty to minorities increases when an aggressive sociopathic individual gains an uncanny, almost hypnotic control over large numbers of people. History is full of chieftains, prophets, saviors, gurus, dictators, and other megalomaniacs who managed to obtain the support from some people in order to enslave them. Almost every historical hero strove to achieve his own immortality and the mortality of other people. Pursuing their allegedly sublime goals, most historical "heroes" fostered hostile feelings and incited to violence. Some of them believed in their historic mission and thought of themselves as saviors; obsessed by delusions of grandeur, overwhelmed by a persecution complex, and driven by an insatiable desire for power, they led millions of people to mass murder and self-destruction. The story of "great" leaders is perhaps the weirdest part of the bizarre history of humanity. Anxiety-ridden individuals, paranoiacs such as Stalin, paranoid schizophrenics such as Tiberius and Calvin, and sociopathic sadists such as Torquemada and Hitler exercised more power than rational leaders.

Some students of social psychology maintain that underprivileged minority groups tend to be more belligerent than others. However, members of the Ku Klux Klan do not belong to an underprivileged minority group nor do the members of various terrorist organizations. Most members of the German Baader-Meinhof gang and of the Italian Red Brigades are middle- or upper-class young people. The parental income of the American SDS, Weathermen, and so on is higher than the average income of parents whose sons and daughters attend Harvard, and the PLO terrorists are well paid and well armed by Saudi Arabia, Syria, Libya, and Iran.

All through human history the persecutors were never members of an underprivileged group. As a rule, the opposite is true. In ancient times the ruling Romans persecuted the Christians, and in medieval times the ruling Christians persecuted the Jews. The persecution of witches was practiced by powerful and self-righteous men against helpless women.

Modern times prove the point too well. Fascists and Nazis

were not a suffering, underprivileged group, and the Russian Bolsheviks persecuted others as soon as they became the ruling clique.

Some researchers pointed out alleged differences in the rate of violent behavior of the various ethnic groups. In the United States the blacks top the list; whereas the black population constitutes 12% of the population, blacks are almost one-half of jail inmates. Victims of a violent assault committed by a single person testified that at least 25% of the attackers were blacks. However, 83% of all cases of physical violence and 70% of all rape cases are committed on people of the same race as the offender, and in World War II many Lithuanians, Poles, Ukrainians, and others successfully competed with the Germans in brutalizing and murdering helpless Jewish men, women, and children.

CURRENT SOCIAL CLIMATE

The present-day sociocultural climate encourages violent behavior. All social relationships and social organizations are based on a partial renunciation of the individual's freedom of action. If this renunciation is voluntary and agreed upon by the participants, it serves as a basis for democracy. Undoubtedly, such a self-restraint by agreement is beneficial to all parties concerned, for it promises the same degree of freedom for all. However, human history is full of sociopaths who demanded all freedom for themselves and no freedom for others. These individuals have tried, often successfully, to impose their will on others and to spread violence and chaos.

It seems that the present-day sociopsychological climate fosters antisocial behavior and genocide, which, with the proliferation of and improvements in weaponry, may mean mass suicide. The two world wars and a host of lesser wars did not cool the aggressive appetites, and the inclination to violent behavior seems to take on epidemic dimensions in international relations and within the boundaries of practically every country.

The United States is not an exception. Atlanta Police Chief Napper said, "There are a lot of young guys who just don't care, who go out and blow people away just for the hell of it" (quoted after *Time*, March 21, 1981). Gates, the Chief of Los Angeles Police, said, "We have lost a whole generation. No self-discipline. Total indulgence. Drugs. Lack of respect for the law. Lack of respect for values. A whole generation thumbed its nose at everything that was held sacred in this country. America has to take a look at its heart and soul" *(ibid.)*. According to Houston Police Chief B. K. Johnson, "We have allowed ourselves to degenerate to the point where we are living like animals. We live behind burglar bars and throw a collection of door locks at night and set an alarm system and lay down with a loaded shotgun beside the bed and then try to get some rest." Chief Justice Warren Burger warned about "the reign of terror in American cities" and asked, "Aren't we hostages within the borders of our own self-styled, enlightened, civilized country?" Dr. J. Wright, Jr., professor of criminology at the Loyola University, maintains that American people lost faith in the judiciary and police system, and they don't believe that police can offer adequate protection for their lives and property. In 1980 nine New York police officers were killed by criminals, and (as mentioned above) in the United States 400 people are murdered every week. Apparently the prevailing sociopsychological climate that removes restraints and inhibitions encourages violence, for many people feel that today it is quite easy "to get away with murder."

DISINHIBITION

Searching for a definition of mental health, I have tried to compare it to physical health. Barring external assaults, people in good health have a good chance for survival. Physical health can therefore be assessed in terms of distance from death; one can put the idea of health in a linear sequence, such as excellent health, good health, poor health, disease, lethal disease, and the final, deadly end—death.

A similar, though not identical approach can be applied in regard to mental health. The struggle for survival is the main and universal aim of all living organisms, and a mentally healthy or "normal" behavior is committed to this goal. Well-adjusted, mentally healthy individuals make optimal use of whatever abilities they have and whatever opportunities they meet, while maladjusted, mentally disturbed individuals are frequently their own worst enemies. One can therefore present the concept of mental health in a linear sequence starting with optimal adjustment, going down to less rational modes of behavior, and ending in a psychotic disarray when mental functions break down. Severe cases of psychoses remove inhibitions, and many psychotics act out their sexual and aggressive impulses and in many instances become a menace to themselves and to others.

There are several aspects of behavior disorders, such as disturbances in cognitive processes, social maladjustment, and inappropriate emotional responses. However, the inability to control one's behavior is an outstanding sign of a severe behavior disorder. One can find in back wards of mental hospitals totally disinhibited individuals who practice sexual freedom and act out aggressive impulses.

One can find in animals and in human neonates disinhibited behavior similar to severe psychosis. A retrospective look into the phylogenetic and ontogenetic aspects of human evolution reveals the roots of psychosis. Judging by comparative-evolutionary standards, psychotic behavior is regressive—that is, as "natural" as the behavior of animals or as natural as the early infantile modes of behavior. Totally uninhibited individuals do not exercise control over their bowels and bladder; they do not practice self-restraint; they bite when hungry; they rape or masturbate when sexually aroused; they attack when annoyed; in short, their "spontaneous" and "natural" behavior knows no limits.

A story has been told about a prominent anthropologist who asked a director of a mental hospital to allow him to spend some time on a ward for research purposes. He wished to be admitted to the hospital as if he were a mental patient and remain in this role undiscovered until the end of his study. He asked the psychiatrist for advice and guidance. The psychiatrist's advice was simple: "Be yourself and act naturally." In other words, follow your impulses and act in a totally uninhibited manner.

Animals and infants act in accordance with their phylogenetic and ontogenetic level of development; the same rule should apply to human adults. Acquisition of culture is a part of the phylogenetic evolution, and the individual's growth through maturation and learning is a part of the ontogenetic evolution. Normal, that is, well-adjusted, individuals are neither as natural as animals nor as immature as infants. They are cultural and mature. Disinhibition and deculturation are signs of regression.

The phylogenetic cultural and the ontogenetic individual maturation are intrinsically interlocked with inhibitions. Culture started when wise men (or God) imposed the "Thou shalt not" rules, for even the most primitive people could not live together without imposing restraint and self-restraint on sexual and aggressive impulses. These restraints have become a part of human nature, and adult individuals are capable of self-control. Culture and inhibition have become their nature.

A tree cannot go back and become a sapling or a seed, but it may become a crippled tree. Renunciation of cultural norms and of self-restraint does not lead back into cribs or jungles: It leads to mental hospitals. Human beings cannot turn the clock back; when they try it, the clock breaks, and severe behavior disorders take place.

In Freud's Victorian times of prudishness and bigotry, hysteria was the most widespread syndrome. In our times of general feelings of insecurity related to economic instability, decline of traditional values, lessening of family ties, and continuous danger of war, many people seem to seek refuge in shallow hedonism and violence, that is, sociopathy.

VIOLENCE AS AN ESCAPE MECHANISM

Violent behavior is often a product of defense mechanisms against inferiority feelings. People who feel secure—that is, have a high estimate of their power—don't have the need or the inclination to use it or to prove that they are strong. However, people who doubt their power may have the need to assert themselves and tend to act aggressively. Hostile behavior, whether offensive or defensive, is not necessarily maladjustive, as long as it serves self-protection and survival (Bandura, 1973). It becomes maladjustive when there is no real threat or when the estimation of the threat is grossly exaggerated.

The feeling of weakness and helplessness makes the sociopaths hate those they could blame for their failures. Hostile behavior and violence are irrational and maladjustive when people overestimate the power of others, misconstrue their intentions, and fear hostility where no hostile action is intended against them.

The more one believes in his power—that is, the more secure one feels—the more one is inclined to act in a magnanimous way. Insecure people are on guard fearing true or imaginary enemies. An insecure mother tends to be punitive, for the child's disobedience presents a threat to her. A secure mother takes lightly the child's temper tantrum; being secure, she can be understanding and magnanimous.

Insecure people admire "heroes" and wish to imitate them. It has always been easier to destroy than to build; destruction requires little effort, endurance, and courage. The so-called "rebellion of youth" was not a genuine effort aimed at improving a faulty social system but rather an infantile temper tantrum. Many children brought up by immature and wishy-washy parents learn to extort concessions by temper tantrums. Insecure parents who fear growing old often try to prevent the growth of their children. Sometimes they prefer to see them taking dope, having "free" sex, and making revolutions rather than joining the adult society as responsible individuals.

The weaker one is, the more secure one feels in a mob, no matter whether the mob is led by religious fanatics, chauvinistic demagogues, or radical zealots. It's easier to fight for peace, religion, social justice, and all the good slogans than to work for them. Violence and destruction give one the much yearned-for illusion of power, while creative efforts make one aware of the limitations of one's power. Roaming mobs and screaming, senseless slogans may give one a feeling of power one does not have.

Ransford (1968) interviewed blacks in the ghetto areas of Watts in Los Angeles. Those blacks who believed themselves to be members of an isolated, powerless minority were quite inclined to commit acts of violence. Inferiority feelings can easily be overcompensated by violence. The fact that one needs little power for destructive actions makes violence attractive to immature, insecure, and maladjusted individuals torn by feelings of inadequacy, inferiority, and weakness.

The frequency of antisocial and violent behavior cannot be explained by a single factor, but it might be related to several sociocultural and socioeconomic factors conducive to widespread feelings of insecurity. Violent behavior often serves as an escape from the feelings of inadequacy, inferiority, and insecurity. Violence on television reduces inhibitions against aggressive behavior. Several articles on aggression in the *International Encyclopedia of Psychiatry, Psychology, Psychoanalysis, and Neurology* (Wolman, 1977) bring evidence that younger children become frightened and develop sleep disturbances and nightmares, while older children and adolescents become disinhibited in their antisocial behavior.

There is no question that some young people who commit crimes of violence have been influenced by frequent and prolonged watching of TV violence.

Violence on television teaches that one can get away with murder. By the age of 18 American youngsters have spent

11,000 hours in schools, but they have watched 18,000 TV murders! Seeing on TV how easy it is to attack innocent people encourages some youngsters to follow the path of crime.

It seems that the present-day sociopsychological climate encourages selfishness and disinhibition. It certainly provides fertile soil for mushrooming of sociopathic personality types and their inclination to violent behavior. Sociopaths are exploitative, and they operate on the principle that weak enemies have to be destroyed and friends are to be used. Their destrudo is highly mobilized and ready to strike against the outer world (object-directed). They perceive themselves as innocent, poor, hungry animals and see other people as actual or potential enemies: "Either you devour them or they devour you." They are highly aggressive, brutal, and cruel to those who fear them, but obedient and subservient to those they fear. In milder cases they appear as selfish individuals; in more severe cases they are cruel criminals who may kill even after they have robbed the victim. They may torture and mutilate their victims because cruelty enhances their feeling of power. They attack, torture, and murder, displaying cruelty and deriving great human pleasure from it.

Sociopaths (I classified them as hyperinstrumental-narcissistic types) are more inclined toward antisocial behavior than any other clinical group. Most of them believe that they are innocent victims of injustice, and they have to defend themselves against a cold and hostile world. When they perpetrate a crime, they believe that they were justified in whatever they did. Sociopaths maintain that their victims were guilty, or they were provoked to act in self-defense, or they had to get even with society, or they were entitled to material gains. Some of them use force for self-aggrandizement or, as they explain it, "for kicks." They often develop paranoid fears and suspect that they are being watched or persecuted. A sociopath caught in the act of theft or robbery may attack maliciously and torture his victims, but when he is undisturbed in his criminal activities or when victims show cooperation, he may abstain from violence. He acts as if saying: "As long as the world recognizes my rights to use others, to loot their possessions, and to enslave them, I shall control my savage impulses, but when the world becomes a threat by denying me my rights, I will not be able to control myself, and my evil impulses may break loose."

RECIDIVISM

Recidivism is typical for the sociopath. According to British research (Gibbens, 1968) close to 60% of hospitalized sociopaths were convicted more than once before and after their hospitalization. Apparently, they do not benefit much from the treatment they receive.

After World War II 14,000 Danish citizens were prosecuted for collaboration with the Nazis during the occupation, and 12,877 men and 644 women were convicted and sentenced to jail. By 1950 about 90% of them were paroled or pardoned. The collaborators were members of the German minority, members of the Danish Nazi party, and Danish non-Nazis. The frequency of pro-Nazi recidivism was 6% among the German minority in Denmark, 10% among the Danish Nazis, and 25% among the non-Nazi collaborators (Christiansen, 1968). The lowest ratio of sociopathic individuals was among people who collaborated with the Germans for reasons somewhat related to ethnic identity. A higher ratio was among those brainwashed to join the Nazi party, and the highest ratio was among the Danish non-Nazis who helped the Germans for personal gain and/or for "kicks."

A sociopath may commit a crime depending on how weak the victim is and how dangerous it is to attack him. Sociopaths avoid hostile behavior when it could be dangerous to themselves; when caught, they regret, not the crime but the punishment. The fear of social disapproval and punishment is the only inhibiting factor that prevents the sociopath from acting out his selfish and antisocial impulses. Sociopaths have no guilt feelings, but they fear punishment.

Fear is probably the sociopaths' main contact with reality. They fear policemen, but only when they see them on guard and well armed. They have no moral judgment, poor perception of reality, and little understanding of potential consequences. Most sociopaths enjoy torturing their victims, derive pleasure out of their sufferings, and get a thrill out of beating, stabbing, and mutilating. They commit artrocities whenever there is an opportunity without retaliation. They may wander aimlessly in a park and attack a lonely woman, a child, or a invalid. They usually rob their victims, but robbery alone does not give them the full amount of feeling of power.

FANATICS AND DICTATORS

One can hardly explain the history of dictatorship as a story of bullets and knives. It must be something in human nature that motivates some individuals to usurp power and other individuals to succumb to such usurpation. There are certain psychological traits common to individuals who crave to control others against their will. The various dictators, the Hitlers and Stalins and the little Jones's of Guyana and other cult leaders, had a similar craving to impose their leadership on others.

I have defined power as the ability to satisfy needs, and acceptance as the willingness to do so. These two dimensions permit one to present social relations as a function of perceiving oneself and others in relation to one's ability to satisfy his or her needs and/or the needs of others and the willingness to do so. Apparently, people perceive themselves as strong or weak, depending on whether they believe that they have the power to satisfy their own needs and the needs of others. The main need of all human beings is survival, and all other needs can be derived from the arch need to stay alive. But since no human being is strong enough to be able to survive without support from without, it is important to have allies. Whether one is surrounded by people who are willing to help in satisfying needs or to destroy him determines the nature of his social relationships. Therefore, one constantly evaluates oneself and others in terms of his own power and the power of the people around him. When one feels that he has adequate power to cope with dangers and has enough friends or allies who are willing to back him, one develops the most important feeling of security.

Well-balanced and self-confident individuals do not need an unconditional surrender of others. Secure individuals accept interdependence; they are willing to satisfy some needs of others and expect to have some of their needs satisfied by them. Well-adjusted individuals are *instrumental* in the sense that they use other people for the satisfaction of their own needs; they are *mutual* in the sense that they relate to some people on a give-and-take basis; they are *vectorial* in the sense that they are willing to satisfy the needs of those who need their help. The balanced individual is instrumental in his bread-winning capacities; he is mutual in sex, marriage, and friendship; and he is vectorial in regard to children and people who need his help. A balanced individual does not have the need to gain control over others. He or she is perfectly satisfied in relating to other people on a give, give-and-take, or take basis; he or she accepts the limitations of his or her power and is satisfied with interdependent relations.

There are, however, individuals who desperately need the feeling of great power because they do not believe they have much power. Those who have adequate faith in themselves and sufficient faith in their friends do not need to have more power than is reasonably necessary for survival and for a reasonable amount of success in life. *But those who doubt themselves and others and who suspect that others are their enemies aspire to gain control over others.* Thus, *badly insecure sociopaths* have no feelings for others. Their self-esteem is exceedingly low, and they believe they are threatened by others and have to defend themselves. A gifted sociopath can assume that kind of leadership and present himself as a poor, innocent martyr. This was, in fact, Hitler's mentality. He spoke of innocent, poor Germany that was defeated in World War I and was threatened by Jews, blacks, British, Frenchmen, Americans, and so on, and had to "defend itself" by mass slaughter of its alleged enemies.

Some dictators believe themselves to be God's gift to earth. Stalin, whose moods shifted from deep depression to great elation, and Mussolini, who was a similar type, inspired the masses by presenting themselves as gods.

Ayatolla Khomeini and his henchmen in Iran terrorize their nation and instigate terrorism in the Middle East, and all over the world. In Northern Ireland, Israel, Italy, Colombia, El Salvador, and everywhere else, terrorist gangs of PLO, Revolutionary Guards, M-19, and other self-styled "freedom fighters" deprive innocent people of *their freedom,* practice self-righteous violence, and murder men, women, and children. Their violent crimes give them a feeling of power and importance.

Many sociopaths practice violence "for kicks," that is, for self-aggrandizement. Violent behavior gives the perpetrators the feeling of power, and sociopaths assault those who cannot defend themselves. Weak and defenseless victims provide the sociopath with a secure and quick victory. Sociopaths are not brave warriors; the terrorists who murdered the lonely American serviceman on a TWA flight after tying him up and the terrorists who murdered an invalid in a wheelchair on a cruise ship were apparently sociopaths who enjoyed a safe and an easy victory over helpless victims.

A psychomotor epileptic or an enraged schizophrenic may singlehandedly launch a self-defeating and potentially suicidal assault, but sociopaths would never attack a strong adversary. Sociopaths tend to join a gang rather than act alone, and many criminal gangs are comprised of sociopaths. (More about this in Chapters 3 and 4.) Many anti-Semitic, antiblack, and any other gangs who persecute minority groups are comprised of sociopaths. Certainly not all Germans were Nazis or pro-Nazis, but a great many Nazis who murdered helpless civilians were selfish, hostile, and cruel sociopaths.

7

Antisocial Behavior in Childhood and Adolescence

CHILDHOOD

Lefkowitz et al. (1977) studied aggressive behavior of 875 third-grade elementary-school children. The children, boys and girls, almost all of them eight years old, were picked at random from a broad ethnic and socioeconomic background in upstate New York. Ten years later a follow-up study supported the original hypothesis; namely, that antisocial violent behavior is a product of environmental influences and of learning process. Parental rejection was found to be related to children's aggressiveness, but the impact of mass media was even more significant. The research adduced adequate evidence that the children's violent behavior was increased whenever they watched violence on television. The conclusions of the research were that the sociocultural climate in the United States was tolerant of and even encouraged violent behavior. In 1973 there were 13,070 gun murders in the United States compared to 85 cases in England and Wales in the same year despite the fact that the United States has only 12 times a bigger population than England and Wales. The violent behavior scores obtained for girls were almost the same as for boys.

One must not overlook the fact that aggressive behavior

could be related not only to sociopathic personality but also to other clinical categories such as developmental disturbances (Curry and Thompson, 1982), minimal brain dysfunction (Loney et al., 1978), and other organic or psychogenic disorders.

As explained in Chapter 1, there is hardly any evidence of a genetic origin of sociopathy, and Chapters 3 and 4 stress the role of sociocultural climate and family in the etiology of sociopathy. Although one need not exclude the possibility of genetic predisposition to be hyperactive and overassertive children, these traits, taken in isolation, could lead to development of active and dynamic personalities who pursue an active and productive life, as well as to development of active, exploitative, and antisocial sociopathy.

There seems to be a high correlation between the feelings of insecurity and inferiority in childhood and the tendency to antisocial and aggressive behavior. As mentioned above, sociopaths tend to believe that they are unfairly treated by everybody and they must overcompensate for their true or imaginary misfortunes.

According to Robins (1974, 1977), the symptoms of a sociopathic personality appear well before the fifteenth year of age. Robins maintained that at least three of the following symptoms appear in childhood: persistent lying, school problems, early drinking, early sexual problems, running away from home, and minor criminal offenses that lead to troubles with police. In adolescence the symptoms become more frequent, especially truancy, sexual transgressions, and trouble with police.

Follow-up Studies

Glueck and Glueck (1959) studied 500 low-social-class boys; their ages ranged from 9 to 17. About 86% of them were arrested for larceny, burglary, or other crimes, and classified as sociopaths. In the following eight-year period, when they were 17–25 years old, 80% of them were arrested at least once and 34% once a year or more often. At the age of 25–31 the rate of arrests declined to 60%. According to Robins (1974), 84% of children referred for antisocial behavior have been years later diagnosed as sociopaths. Thus, the "distinction between antisocial (sociopathic) and other maladjustment outcomes is predicted by higher frequency and seriousness of antisocial behavior in children who later are diagnosed as sociopathic" (Kohlberg et al., 1972, p. 1253).

Continuity of antisocial behavior and persistent recidivism after hospitalization, jail, and *even* treatment seems to be typical for sociopathic school-age children (Gibbens, 1968).

ADOLESCENCE

In many instances the antisocial behavior erupts in adolescence. The transition from childhood into adulthood is not an easy task in any society, but the complexity of modern societies creates additional difficulties. The age of physical maturation has not changed much in the course of millennia, but the time of psychosocial maturity has undergone substantial changes.

Physical and sexual maturity is attained today at the age of 15–18 for boys and 13–16 for girls, but boys and girls in their teens are unable to support themselves nor are they capable of assuming responsibility for family relationships. A technological society has no use for juvenile shepherds and hunters, and the modern economic system is based on skilled labor and highly qualified managerial and professional cadres. A grade-school dropout can hardly earn a living in our society, and there are fewer and fewer job opportunities for unskilled labor. Prolonged schooling is needed for economic adjustment, and adequate psychocultural maturity is a prerequisite for an adult participation in modern societies. A socioeconomic-cultural maturity requires a high-level psychological development which can hardly be attained in the teens.

This descrepancy between biopsychological and sociocultural maturity is aggravated by several factors. One of them is inherent in the biochemical changes in young age accompanied by an abundance of physical and mental energy, aggressiveness, and frequent overestimation of their own potentialities. Adolescent and postadolescent years are a period of frequent conflicts, for young people tend to believe that they are adult and should, therefore, be granted the status of adults.

This process of self-assertion leads to a normal breaking away from parental authority. Adolescence is the first period of this rebellion; late teens and postadolescence is the second period. The first step is, usually, wholly negative; adolescents may try to do whatever seems to be contrary to parental wishes; they may break, intentionally, parental prohibitions and indulge in juvenile pranks, while still depending economically and psychologically on their parents.

A "rebellion" against dependence does not make anyone independent but dependable, that is, adult. Young men and women who are gainfully employed and, eventually, marry and take care of their children are adults. They assume adult responsibilities, thus they become adult. They don't have to "kill" their fathers to become fathers themselves, but they finally resolve their Oedipal attachments by taking over the adult roles.

The adolescent's self-image depends on peer approval. Almost all adolescents seek popularity and fear rejection. Their hair style, clothes, speech, and several aspects of their behavior conform to the standards of their peer group.

Delinquent behavior is not uncommon even in normal adolescents, and a great many adolescent boys are involved in delinquent activities. The relative prevalence of delinquent acts in adolescence is a reminder of the phase-specific rebelliousness of adolescents.

Violent deaths (caused by accidents, homicide, and suicide) are the leading cause of death in adolescence. The adolescent inclination for reckless car driving is a significant factor in the high rate of accidental deaths in adolescence. The high incidence of violence and self-destructive behaviors proves that adolescence is a period of activation of powerful drives and intensified narcissistic attitudes.

Aggressive Behavior

Most adolescents tend to act impulsively, and whenever provoked, annoyed, or frustrated, they act out their anger and become aggressive (Keith, 1984). There is, however, a distinct difference between the occasional acting-out followed by guilt feelings and the behavior of sociopathic adolescents who hurt others and experience no guilt feelings whatsoever. Mosher et al. (1980), in their research conducted on college students, have drawn a distinction between those who believe that aggression is immoral and experience guilt feelings and those who have low or no guilt feelings. Probably the no-guilt-feeling individuals could be classified as sociopaths.

Sociopathic adolescents, boys and girls alike, practice indiscriminate aggressive behavior. It is not necessarily a reaction to frustration nor is it elicited by anger. Their aggressive behavior gives them a pleasurable feeling of power (Anchor & Cross, 1974; Frank & Quinlan, 1976; Wolman, 1973).

Adolescent Murderers

Not all adolescent murderers are sociopaths, but only sociopaths commit a calculated, cold-blooded murder. Sociopathic adolescents harbor resentment against whoever does not satisfy their narcissistic needs. The annual frequency of homicides by male adolescents is 5% per 100,000 population and slightly below 0.5% by female adolescents (Smith et al., 1980).

The diagnostic evaluations are not definite, but about 40% of adolescent murderers are believed to be paranoid schizophrenics and another 40% sociopaths. Organic brain syndrome, psychomotor epilepsy, and minimal brain dysfunction are also potential causes. In a study reported by Allison and Harmala (1981), 42% of the adolescent murderers were paranoid schizophrenics and 39% sociopaths.

Parental brutality and provocations are quite often the last and the fatal incentive. Some disturbed parents excessively mistreat the child, who eventually develops into a sociopathic, antisocial personality and acts out his or her rage against the persecuting parent. Some school-age children exposed to parental violence tend to direct their rage against the parents and other people. Many of them become adolescent murderers.

Aichhorn (1935) related violent behavior in adolescence to an unresolved Oedipal wish to kill one's parent and to the resulting feeling of guilt. Another psychoanalyst, Glover (1960), interpreted adolescent homicide as an attack on alleged persecutors and wish to be punished—all related to guilt feeling stemming from the unresolved Oedipal conflict.

Violent behavior in children and adolescents is often related to sociocultural climate in their close environment. According to Sorrels (1980), many adolescent murderers live in an environment where human life is not highly valued.

Adolescent parricide is quite often a direct reaction to parental abuse and brutality. In some instances the physical interparental violence serves as a role model. I had in treatment a young man who witnessed in childhood frequent physical fights between his parents. Once his 16-year-old sister borrowed the mother's high-heel shoes to go to a party. When the girl came home, the mother grabbed the shoes and split the girl's skull with the high heel. Whenever the father brutally assaulted the mother, the mother told the 15-year-old boy that "he is not a man" unless he would take a knife and stab his father.

8

Juvenile Delinquency

SOCIAL INFLUENCES

Juvenile delinquency did not start in our times. Over six thousand years ago an Egyptian priest carved in stone the following words:

> Our earth is degenerate:
> Children no longer obey their parents.

The term juvenile delinquency was coined almost 100 years ago, in 1899, when the state of Illinois established the Court for Juvenile Offenders.

A. Johnson (1959) introduced a distinction between "sociological" and "individual" delinquents. "Sociological delinquents" are not pathological; they merely come from a sociocultural background that does not accept the legal and moral standards of the society-at-large, but it condones antisocial and criminal behavior. The "individual delinquents" are brought up by disturbed parents.

One may go one step further in drawing a distinction between psychopathology and group pressure. Many Nazis and most of their leaders were definitely sociopaths, delighted to display their power. They tortured innocent people without ever having any feelings of guilt and remorse. However, many Germans who took part in the savagery were not innocent followers, but would not practice cruelties on their own initiative. Some members and many leaders of juvenile delinquency groups and terrorist organizations are sociopaths who thrive on cruelty and violence, but some of them are uncritical gang followers.

Epstein (1962) compared the *self-image* of delinquents and nondelinquents. He used the Russell Sage Foundation questionnaire sponsored by a research team studying the "Influence of the Self-Image on Academic and Career Achievement." The social agencies chose girls aged 14–18 years who were expected to eventually break the law and whose behavior had already been brought to the attention of the Children's Court, school authorities, and parents. The antisocial behavior of the delinquent girls included sexual offenses, gang activities, shoplifting, and assault and battery. Twenty-one girls were chosen, most of whom were under treatment in some social organization. There were five blacks and 16 whites, 14 Jewish and 7 Protestant girls. Included in the group were 18 girls from broken homes.

The control sample of nondelinquent girls was drawn randomly from a previously tested sample of 286 high-school juniors. They came from a Connecticut, predominantly Catholic suburb with a low delinquency ratio. Eighteen of the girls came from intact families and three came from broken homes.

The girls were asked to describe themselves the way they were at the time, and as they hoped to be in the future and to compare the two in both importance and acceptability. Their aspirations were rated on emotional stability and realism of the level of their goals. In addition, they were asked to describe the support of their goals by parents and peers. There were two bases for comparison of the groups: first, the content of the self-concept, and second, the structural properties of the self-concept.

The results of the tests were quite different from what

had been expected. There were no significant differences in the two groups with regard to stability and realistic expectation levels. In addition, the environmental support was about the same for both groups.

The self-concept was classified under five headings: (1) social groups and classifications, (2) ideological beliefs, (3) interests, (4) ambitions, and (5) self-evaluations. The answers given by the two groups indicated that the delinquents gave more self-evaluative responses, while the average group gave more group-oriented responses. Furthermore, the answers given by the delinquent group conveyed a negative self-evaluation, whereas the answers given by the nondelinquent group were much more positive.

The research pointed to the considerable difference in the content of the self-concept, namely, that delinquents' self-concept reflects a high degree of negativism. Their self-evaluation was indicative of feelings of isolation, loneliness, and rejection, typical for delinquents. Apparently, delinquents cannot cope with their emotional needs or suppress them, and they lack the ability to adjust themselves to social demands.

A good self-concept, which is usually a result of adequate socialization, counteracts the temptation of slum teen-agers to join a delinquent gang. A poor self-concept offers the slum adolescents very little or no resistance to associate with delinquent companions. A good self-concept, indicative of a strong superego and realistic attitudes, steers the adolescents away from delinquent companions and street-corner society toward middle-class values. It encourages the adolescent's efforts to move up in all aspects of his life (Thrasher, 1930; Whyte, 1943).

SEX DIFFERENCES IN DELINQUENCY

Boys are usually involved in burglary, theft, robbery, and car theft. Girls are generally involved in incorrigibility, sexual offenses, and running away from home. While the boy becomes delinquent in order to gain status recognition, the girl is delinquent in an attempt to gratify her needs or to rid herself of hostile feelings. Studies of institutionalized delinquents indicate that the majority of juveniles committed to training schools come from highly disorganized and broken home settings, and there is a high correlation between school failure and delinquency. However, this is not due to the fact that a delinquent is necessarily lower in intelligence than a nondelinquent. Many girls have a higher rate of failure in school because they strike out against school authority and are more easily discouraged.

SOCIAL CLASS VARIABLES

Differences between specific factors in delinquency in the various classes have been studied by several writers. Erikson and Empey (1965) found in their study that the upper-class group was significantly less inclined than the other two to have delinquent associations, but there was no difference between middle- and lower-class boys.

Lower-class delinquents usually view themselves as being tougher, more fearless, more powerful, and more dangerous, while middle-class boys feel that they are smarter, bad, and more daring.

In a study of differential socioeconomic effects, Stanfield (1966) found that at a lower socioeconomic level the delinquency is related to parental rejection and lack of discipline. Myerhoff and Myerhoff (1964) found that middle-class adolescents displayed extreme conformity to the peer group in dress and they exhibited carefully planned elegant casualness.

Possession of a car influences the teenager's social life. Quite often the size of a group is determined by the number of individuals that a single car can hold. The car is their mobile parlor, clubhouse, dining room, and bedroom and influences the teen-agers' sociability and sexuality.

Deviant activities in the "middle-class gang" range from

curfew violations and beer drinking to theft and drugs. Those more serious acts are, however, rarely performed as a group; theft is the most common serious offense, and automobile theft is usually prevalent in the middle-class gangs. The antisocial activities are for the most part nonviolent; physical aggression is rare. Middle- and upper-class delinquents are more likely to be involved in drinking parties, traffic violations, and joy riding as opposed to mugging or gang wars of low-socioeconomic-class delinquents.

It must be added at this point that antisocial behavior is not typical for all adolescents. Only some of them, most probably sociopathic individuals, turn to practice extreme selfishness, disregard for the rights of other people, and reject the socially accepted restraints and regulations.

The most frequent middle-class delinquent activities are truancy, speeding, illegal purchase and consumption of alcohol, and sex. As long as these activities remain within certain bounds, they are often viewed as typical for adolescents. The adolescents and their parents tend to take a permissive attitude and view these activities as adolescent pranks and not as a violation of the law.

The disparity between what lower-class youth craves and what is available to them is a significant cause of maladjustment. Unable and unwilling to revise their aspirations downward, the low-socioeconomic-class youngsters are tempted to act in a nonconformist and antisocial manner.

A. K. Cohen (1955) stressed the role of the subcultural behavioral patterns of the lower socioeconomic classes. Cohen distinguished five factors that lead to the development of subculture: (1) *economic differences,* which lead to (2) *class and social stratification,* which gives rise to (3) *status frustration* in the lower classes. The frustration in turn leads to (4) *reaction formation* (rebellion) against middle-class norms, and therefore, the members of the lower class adopt (5) *deviant norms.* Cohen (1955) says: "The hallmark of the delinquent subculture is the explicit and wholesale repudiation of middle-class standards and the adoption of their very antithesis"

(p. 129). The middle-class norms that are rejected include ambition, individual responsibility, cultivation of skills, postponement of gratification, rationality, good manners, control of physical aggression, wholesome use of leisure, and respect for property. The members of the delinquent subculture manifest their attitude of rebelliousness, malice, negativism, and excessive hedonism.

Spergel (1967) says the delinquent subculture arises in response to (1) lower-class culture and (2) the basic youth culture. It represents an attempt to deal with such everyday problems as broken homes, chronic or seasonal unemployment, inadequate housing, and limited education. The larger problem is of being caught between childhood dependence and adult independence, and the gang becomes an insular world which gives the adolescents a sense of security.

Marshall and Mason (1968) proposed two factors with which to classify populations: (1) the degree of congruence of the adult and juvenile social systems, that is, the extent to which the younger generation accepts the values, attitudes, and behavior patterns of the adult social system in which they grow up, and (2) density of personal relationships, that is, the extent and quality of close relations outside the nuclear family.

Using these two concepts, Marshall and Mason distinguish four types of populations: (1) High-congruence and low-density middle class and some members of the working class. These people are more concerned with personal success than with interpersonal relations, and delinquency is rather limited. (2) High-congruence and high-density working-class community. (3) Low-congruence and high-density population where broken and demoralized families live. This type of community probably corresponds to those in which the violent, conflict-oriented behavior develops. (4) Low-congruence, high-density refers to the gang neighborhood, where the adult culture exerts little influence and interpersonal relations are of a peer group.

This classification system relates significantly with the socialization process, for in categories 1 and 2 the families are quite influential, while in 3 there is little consistent socialization, and in 4 the peer group is the socializing agency. In category 4 the individuals are blocked in their efforts to achieve their goals and might resort to antisocial behavior. In category 2 delinquency corresponds to the lower-class subculture, which is more tolerant of delinquent behavior. A sense of lawlessness could be the cause of delinquency in category 3, while in category 4 the adolescents' behavior follows the prevailing adolescent subculture.

THE ROLE OF PARENTS

During the period of transition in the United States from the agrarian society to the urban industrial society, profound changes took place in the function of the family. A considerable decline in social control over childhood seems to be related to the growth of juvenile delinquency. Losses of family control have been associated with far-reaching changes in the relationships between parents and children. The nineteenth-century American family was paternalistic and authoritarian. In the last few decades paternal authority has given way either to a maternal authority or to no authority whatsoever. Contemporary adolescents and even children have become guides and leaders in matters of conduct and conformity. The exaggerated emphasis on child-centered education and the disorganization in American family life have contributed in a marked degree to a disrespect for the rights of other people and a growing spirit of license.

It is still an open question whether broken homes or disturbed homes cause more serious psychological harm to the children. Often a broken home with one parent can offer a child a more stable environment than a home with two quarreling parents! In both disorganized and broken homes the lines of communication are cut off, which leads to a failure to learn appropriate social values. Many children from broken homes tend to act out their tensions in hostile and destructive manners.

In a report to the WHO (World Health Organization) Gibbens (1968) pointed to the role of maternal domination in delinquent homes. In many homes that breed delinquency, the father, for work or for other reasons, plays a reduced role in the family life, and the mother takes over the function of providing affection and discipline. The teen-age boy who has identified with the mother and relied on her as a "role model" may have difficulty in shaping a masculine self-concept and tends to be aggressive in an attempt to "prove" his masculinity.

According to Andry (1962), delinquent boys feel rejected by their fathers but loved by their mother, while nondelinquents feel loved by both parents. Several researchers have pointed to the high incidence of maladjusted fathers of delinquent boys (Glueck & Glueck, 1962). Alcoholism, brutality, antisocial attitudes, failure to provide, frequent absences from home, and other characteristics made the father an inadequate and unacceptable identification model for the boy. Sociopathic fathers also contribute to antisocial behavior in their daughters, including covert encouragement of sexual promiscuity.

JUVENILE GANGS

It must be stated that not all sociopathic adolescents violate the existing laws and therefore should be classified as delinquents, nor are all juvenile delinquents sociopathic personalities. However, whereas nonsociopathic adolescents might commit crimes, they usually experience feelings of guilt and remorse. Many nonsociopathic adolescents join an antisocial gang to avoid being lonely and eventually ostracized.

One of the chief traits of adolescent groups is "that they have no set platforms, programs, or official membership requirements. . . . each member determines his own role, with leadership depending upon the focus of interest at a specific time" (Robinson, 1965, p. 122). The members of a

New York City gang in a Harlem neighborhood engaged in playing stickball, gambling, and unrestricted sexual activities. Occasionally they drank, smoked marijuana, stole, and fought with other gangs usually for the purpose of being "tough."

Juvenile gangs were studied by Thrasher (1930), Whyte (1943), Spergel (1967), Yablonsky (1962), and many others.

Spergel (1967) described three types of delinquent gangs: (1) The racket group organized play groups in areas where the racket subculture predominates. The racket gangs are usually well organized, homogeneous, and directly influenced by older gang groups with criminal backgrounds. The members of the racket groups spend most of their time in petty delinquency and in helping racketeers. These gangs practice solidarity with criminal norms and values and are involved in illegitimate activities. (2) The theft gangs start in an area of theft subculture. These gangs are not as homogeneous as the racket gangs and experience more individual than group-oriented interaction. The activities of theft gangs consist of various kinds of theft, with delinquent behavior becoming increasingly directed to criminal behavior as members become older. Aggression is limited to fist fights among members or directed against adults. (3) The conflict groups are usually most destructive; they originate at the lowest class areas. The members of the conflict gangs are usually individuals of minority groups. Relationships to the family, to other individuals, or to society are practically nonexistent. The conflict groups are not cohesive except at times of gang fight.

Yablonsky (1962) described three types of juvenile gangs as follows:

> ... the *delinquent gang* is dominated by delinquent patterns of activities characterized by such direct illegal behavior as stealing or assault with material profit as the essential objective; the *violent gang's* activity is dominated by sociopathic themes of spontaneous prestige-seeking violence with psychic gratification (kicks) as the goal; the *social gang* is a social group comprised of tough youths who band together because

they believe and find their individual goals of a socially constructive nature can most adequately be achieved through their gang pattern. (p. 149)

According to Yablonsky, the contemporary form of the gangs reflects a brand and intensity of violence that differentiates it from earlier gang patterns. The "kill for kicks" homicide is today a source of concern, not only in the large city (11 gang homicides in New York City in the summer of 1978) but also in the suburbs and the small towns.

Obviously, the members of the gangs are typical sociopaths. The New York City Youth Board (1960) has studied the structure and dynamics of juvenile gangs and reported 12 needs for which the individual finds satisfaction in the gang:

1) His need to convince himself that he is a person of worth.
2) His need for acceptance, belonging and recognition.
3) His need for new experiences, shared interest and ideals.
4) The need for common support on a peer level in a subculture of society toward which tremendous punitiveness, hostility and conflict is directed.
5) The need to possess, to own and control.
6) The need for status in the neighborhood and community in which he lives.
7) The need to identify with something in the subculture which symbolized power, authority and prestige.
8) The need to have an impersonal mechanism through which he can rebel against environment, both physically and socially; to deal with and express his fears, anxieties, insecurities, as well as those feelings of hostility, aggression and anger.
9) The need for protection from real or fantasized threats.
10) The need for opportunity for sublimating and expressing basic drives.

11) The need for peer group-evolved concepts of equality, justice and control.
12) The teenage need for symbolic group ceremonies and activities. (pp. 18–19)

According to Yablonsky (1962), (1) the violent gang is devoid of stable social role positions—even the position of the leader is less stable and visible than is usually believed; (2) the structure of violent gangs is mostly related to its members' age, school attendance, and proximity to accepted hangouts; (3) the violent gangs are not organized around specific tasks; (4) the cohesiveness of the gang is usually a function of withdrawal from outside sources of frustration and perceived threat from outside; (5) the turnover rate of gang membership is quite high; some members of the gang take part in certain activities in response to their instant emotional needs; (6) gang leaders are usually severely disturbed sociopaths who use the gang to fulfill their own needs.

PART III

Theoretical Viewpoints

9

Psychiatric Manuals and Other Theories

Researchers have offered various theories concerning the etiology of sociopathic personality. Apparently, there is no agreement as to what causes sociopathy or what are the dynamics of sociopathic behavior. A brief review of the three editions of the *Diagnostic and Statistical Manual of Mental Disorders of the American Psychiatric Association*, the DSM-I (1952), the DSM-II (1968), and the DSM-III (1980), will point out the controversial issues, as presented by the psychiatric classification systems.

The DSM-I (1952) described the sociopathic personality disorder as follows:

> [Individuals with] Sociopathic Personality are ill primarily in terms of society and of conformity with the prevailing cultural milieu, and not only in terms of personal discomfort and relations with other individuals. However, sociopathic reactions are very often symptomatic of severe underlying personality disorder, neurosis, or psychosis, or occur as the result of organic brain injury or disease. Before definitive diagnosis in this group is employed, strict attention must be paid to the possibility of the presence of a more primary personality disturbance. . . .
> Antisocial Reaction . . . refers to chronically antisocial individuals who are always in trouble, profiting neither from experience nor punishment, and maintaining no real loyalties

to any person, group or code. They are frequently callous and hedonistic, showing marked emotional immaturity, with lack of sense of responsibility, lack of judgment, and ability to rationalize their behavior so that it appears warranted, reasonable, and justified. . . . The term includes cases previously classified as "constitutional psychopathic state" and "psychopathic personality." As defined here the term is more limited, as well as more specific in its application. . . .

Dyssocial Reaction . . . applies to individuals who manifest disregard for the usual social codes, and often come in conflict with them, as the result of having lived all their lives in an abnormal moral environment. They may be capable of strong loyalties. These individuals typically do not show significant personality deviations other than those implied by adherence to the values or code of their own predatory, criminal, or other social group. The term includes such diagnoses as "pseudosocial personality" and "psychopathic personality with asocial and amoral trends."

The DSM-II (1968) introduced three different types of sociopaths, namely, (1) antisocial behavior, (2) passive-aggressive personality, and (3) dyssocial behavior. And here these three categories are described:

1) Antisocial Personality—This term is reserved for individuals who are basically unsocialized and whose behavior pattern brings them repeatedly into conflict with society. They are incapable of significant loyalty to individuals, groups or social values. They are grossly selfish, callous, irresponsible, impulsive, and unable to feel guilt or to learn from experience and punishment. Frustration tolerance is low. They tend to blame others or offer plausible rationalizations for their behavior. A mere history of repeated legal or social offenses is not sufficient to justify this diagnosis. Group delinquent reaction of childhood (or adolescence), and Social Maladjustment without manifest psychiatric disorder should be ruled out before making this diagnosis.

2) Passive-Aggressive Personality—This behavior pattern is characterized by both passivity and aggressiveness. The aggressiveness may be expressed passively, for example, by obstructionism, pouting, procrastination, intentional inefficiency, or stubbornness. This behavior commonly reflects hostility which the individual feels but he dare not express openly. Often the behavior is an expression of the patient's resentment at failing to find gratification in a relationship with an individual or institution upon which he is over-dependent.

3) *Dyssocial Behavior*—This category is for individuals who are not classifiable as anti-social personalities, but who are predatory and follow more or less criminal pursuits, such as racketeers, dishonest gamblers, prostitutes and dope peddlers. [DSM-I classified this condition as "sociopathic personality disorder, dyssocial type."]

The DSM-III (1980) suggested four types of sociopaths under the heading conduct disorders. The four types are (1) undersocialized, nonaggressive disorders, (2) undersocialized, aggressive, (3) socialized, aggressive, and (4) socialized, non-aggressive. A description of the four categories follows:

> The *Undersocialized* types are characterized by a failure to establish a normal degree of affection, empathy, or bond with others. Peer relationships are generally lacking, although the youngster may have superficial relationships with other youngsters. Characteristically, the child does not extend himself or herself for others unless there is an obvious immediate advantage. Egocentrism is shown by readiness to manipulate others for favors without any effort to reciprocate. There is generally a lack of concern for the feelings, wishes, and well-being of others, as shown by callous behavior. Appropriate feelings of guilt or remorse are generally absent. Such a child may readily inform on his or her companions and try to place blame on them.
>
> The *Socialized* types show evidence of social attachment to others, but may be similarly callous or manipulative toward persons to whom they are not attached and lack guilt when these "outsiders" are made to suffer.
>
> The *Aggressive* types are characterized by a repetitive and persistent pattern of aggressive conduct in which the rights of others are violated, by either physical violence against persons, or thefts outside the home involving confrontation with a victim. The physical violence may take the form of rape, mugging, assault, or in rare cases, homicide. In some cases, the physical violence may be directed against parents.

Thefts outside the home may involve extortion, purse snatching, or holdup of a store.

The *Nonaggressive* types are characterized by the absence of physical violence against persons and of robbery outside the home involving confrontation with a victim. However, there is a persistent pattern of conduct in conflict with norms for their age, which may take the form of: chronic violations of a variety of important rules that are reasonable and age-appropriate for the child at home or at school, such as persistent truancy and substance abuse; running away from home overnight while living in the parental home; persistent serious lying in and out of the home; vandalism or fire-setting; or stealing (not involving confrontation of a victim).

Associated features (all four types). Difficulties at home and in the community are common. Frequently there is precocious sexual activity, which may be aggressive or submissive, depending on subtype. The child typically blames others for his or her difficulties and feels unfairly treated and mistrustful of others. Self-esteem is usually low, though the individual may project an image of "toughness." Unusually early smoking, drinking, and other substance use are also common. Poor frustration tolerance, irritability, temper outbursts, and provocative recklessness are often present. Academic achievement is frequently below the level expected on the basis of intelligence and age. Attentional difficulties are common and may justify the additional diagnosis of Attention Deficit Disorder. One or more Specific Developmental Disorders may be present.

In the Socialized types, sometimes there is membership in a gang and the antisocial behavior may be limited to gang activities.

Age at onset. Onset is usually prepubertal for the Undersocialized type and pubertal or postpubertal for the Socialized type.

Course. The course is variable, mild forms frequently showing improvement over time and severe forms tending to be chronic. Some individuals may continue their antisocial behavior and generally poor social functioning into adulthood, particularly the Undersocialized, Aggressive type, and thus qualify for the diagnosis of Antisocial Personality Disorder. Others may display adequate social functioning but persist in illegal activity, and may be considered to have Adult Antisocial Behavior. Finally, many achieve reasonable social and occupational adjustment as adults, particularly the Socialized, Nonaggressive type.

Impairment. The degree of impairment varies from mild to severe. It may preclude attendance in the ordinary school classroom or living at home or in a foster home. When antisocial behavior is extreme, institutionalization, with its temporary loss of autonomy, may be necessary.

Complications. Complications include school suspension, legal difficulties, Substance Use Disorders, venereal diseases, unwanted pregnancy, high rate of physical injury from accidents, fights along with retaliation by victims, and suicidal behavior.

Predisposing factors. Attention Deficit Disorder, parental rejection, inconsistent management with harsh discipline, early institutional living, frequent shifting of parent figures (foster parents, relatives, or stepparents), and being an illegitimate only child may predispose to the development of the Undersocialized type. Large family size, association with a delinquent subgroup, and an absent father or a father with Alcohol Dependence may predispose to the development of the Socialized type.

Prevalence. The disorder is common, particularly the Socialized, Nonaggressive and the Undersocialized, Aggressive types.

Sex ratio. The disorder is far more common among boys than among girls, the ratios ranging from 4:1 to 12:1. The only exception may be the Undersocialized, Nonaggressive type, which may be equally common in both sexes.

Familial pattern. The disorder is more common in children of adults with Antisocial Personality Disorder and Alcohol Dependence than in the general population.

Differential diagnosis. Isolated acts of antisocial behavior do not justify a diagnosis of Conduct Disorder and may be coded as Childhood or Adolescent Antisocial Behavior. The behavior qualifies for a diagnosis of Conduct Disorder only if the antisocial behavior represents a repetitive and persistent pattern. When such a pattern exists there will usually be obvious impairment in social and school functioning that frequently will not be present when the antisocial behavior represents an isolated act.

In *Oppositional Disorder* there are some of the features that are present in Conduct Disorder, such as disobedience and opposition to authority figures. However, the basic rights of others and major age-appropriate societal norms or rules are not violated as they are in Conduct Disorder.

Attention Deficit Disorder and *Specific Developmental Disorder* are common associated diagnoses, and should also be noted when present.

DIAGNOSTIC CRITERIA—CONDUCT DISORDER, UNDERSOCIALIZED, AGGRESSIVE

A. A repetitive and persistent pattern of aggressive conduct in which the basic rights of others are violated, as manifested by either of the following:
  1) physical violence against persons or property (not to defend someone else or oneself), e.g., vandalism, rape, breaking and entering, fire-setting, mugging, assault
  2) thefts outside the home involving confrontation with the victim (e.g., extortion, purse-snatching, armed robbery)
B. Failure to establish a normal degree of affection, empathy, or bond with others as evidenced by *no more than one* of the following indications of social attachment:
  1) has one or more peer-group friendships that have lasted over six months
  2) extends himself or herself for others even when no immediate advantage is likely
  3) apparently feels guilt or remorse when such a reaction is appropriate (not just when caught or in difficulty)
  4) avoids blaming or informing on companions
  5) shares concern for the welfare of friends or companions
C. Duration of pattern of aggressive conduct of at least six months.
D. If 18 or older, does not meet the criteria for Antisocial Personality Disorder.

DIAGNOSTIC CRITERIA—CONDUCT DISORDER, UNDERSOCIALIZED, NONAGGRESSIVE

A. A repetitive and persistent pattern of nonaggressive conduct in which either the basic rights of others or major age-appropriate societal norms or rules are violated, as manifested by any of the following:

1) chronic violations of a variety of important rules (that are reasonable and age-appropriate for the child) at home or at school (e.g., persistent truancy, substance abuse)
2) repeated running away from home overnight
3) persistent serious lying in and out of the home
4) stealing not involving confrontation with a victim

B. Failure to establish a normal degree of affection, empathy, or bond with others as evidenced by *no more than one* of the following indications of social attachment:
1) has one or more peer-group friendships that have lasted over six months
2) extends himself or herself for others even when no immediate advantage is likely
3) apparently feels guilt or remorse when such a reaction is appropriate (not just when caught or in difficulty)
4) avoids blaming or informing on companions
5) shows concern for the welfare of friends or companions

C. Duration of pattern of nonaggressive conduct of at least six months.

D. If 18 or older, does not meet the criteria for Antisocial Personality Disorder.

DIAGNOSTIC CRITERIA—CONDUCT DISORDER, SOCIALIZED, AGGRESSIVE

A. A repetitive and persistent pattern of aggressive conduct in which the basic rights of others are violated, as manifested by either of the following:
1) physical violence against persons or property (not to defend someone else or oneself), e.g., rape, breaking and entering, fire-setting, mugging, assault
2) thefts outside the home involving confrontation with a victim (e.g., extortion, purse-snatching, armed robbery)

B. Evidence of social attachment to others as indicated by at least two of the following behavior patterns:
1) has one or more peer-group friendships that have lasted over six months
2) extends himself or herself for others even when no immediate advantage is likely
3) apparently feels guilt or remorse when such a reaction is appropriate (not just when caught or in difficulty)

4) avoids blaming or informing on companions
   5) shows concern for the welfare of friends or companions
C. Duration of pattern of aggressive conduct of at least six months.
D. If 18 or older, does not meet the criteria for Antisocial Personality Disorder.

DIAGNOSTIC CRITERIA—CONDUCT DISORDER, SOCIALIZED, NONAGGRESSIVE

A. A repetitive and persistent pattern of nonaggressive conduct in which either the basic rights of others or major age-appropriate societal norms or rules are violated, as manifested by any of the following:
   1) chronic violations of a variety of important rules that are reasonable and age-appropriate for the child) at home or at school (e.g., persistent truancy, substance abuse)
   2) repeated running away from home overnight
   3) persistent serious lying in and out of the home
   4) stealing not involving confrontation with a victim
B. Evidence of social attachment to others as indicated by at least two of the following behavior patterns:
   1) has one or more peer-group friendships that have lasted over six months
   2) extends himself or herself for others even when no immediate advantage is likely
   3) apparently feels guilt or remorse when such a reaction is appropriate (not just when caught or in difficulty)
   4) avoids blaming or informing on companions
   5) shows concern for the welfare of friends or companions
C. Duration of pattern of nonaggressive conduct of at least six months
D. If 18 or older, does not meet the criteria for Antisocial Personality Disorder. (DSM-III, 1980, pp. 45-50)

OTHER THEORIES

Pritchard maintained that the antisocial sociopaths are morally insane. In 1835 Pritchard described moral insanity as follows: "The power of self-government is lost or greatly impaired in the individual who is found to be incapable not of talking or reasoning on any subject proposed to him, but of conducting himself in decency and propriety in the business of life."

As mentioned in Chapter 1, Lombroso (1911) maintained that antisocial behavior is inherited. Glueck and Glueck (1956, 1959, 1962) followed in Lombroso's footsteps and related antisocial and delinquent behavior to inherited anatomical and physiological traits. They maintained that the physical constitution (physique) is the primary and fundamental factor reinforced by family environment and sociocultural influences. Glueck and Glueck put more emphasis on organic determinants, whereas other research workers stressed psychological and sociopsychological issues.

According to McCord and McCord (1956, 1964), the sociopaths are asocial individuals. They have no capacity for love for anyone except themselves and have no feeling of guilt no matter how much harm they do to others. They treat other people as objects to be used and abused. Their antisocial aggressive and impulsive behavior is evident in childhood when they display cruelty to other children and animals.

The sociopaths are always in search of a change, always expecting to find greener pastures. They have no stable goals, except the continuous goal of their own satisfaction and pleasure. Their uninhibited search for unrestricted pleasure leads to frequent conflicts with other people; when other people refuse to be used, the frustrated sociopaths tend to become furious and quite aggressive.

Bright psychopaths (the terms sociopath and psychopath are used interchangeably) are capable of pretending to feel guilty and profess remorse. They often talk of morality, but they feel none. Usually their words mean nothing and do not prevent their actions, and serve as cover-ups for their antisocial behavior.

Most psychopaths are quite sensitive to social pressures and crave approval. Usually they follow the superficial and obvious manners of our culture and abide by certain sociocultural rules. They brush their teeth, obviously drive on the right side of the road, and wear appropriate clothes. They believe they are innocent, law-abiding, and fair-minded individuals. They may attend churches and synagogues and pretend to strictly follow the socially accepted norms, but their actions are antisocial, hostile, and aggressive.

"If society has the will, it can protect itself against this most dangerous and, at the same time, most lonely of all human beings," McCord and McCord concluded in their book *The Psychopath: An Essay on the Criminal Mind* (1964).

Cleckley, in the early edition of his book *The Mask of Sanity*, expressed the belief that the psychopathic personality was a psychotic disorder, probably a subtype of schizophrenia. In the 1976 edition of his book, Cleckley wrote:

> In the psychopath, we maintain there is also a generalized abnormality or defect of the personality that can be compared with schizophrenia, in contrast with ordinary psychoneurosis. . . . It cannot be said that the disorder is that of schizophrenia, but in the whole of the patient's life, we find such inadequacy of response, such failure of the adaptation, that it seems plausible to postulate alterations more fundamental and more extensive than in classic psychoneuroses. . . . It is offered (here) as an opinion that a real pathology is general, and that the psychopath is more closely aligned with the psychotic than with the psychoneurotic patient. The pathology may be regarded not as gross fragmentation of the personality but as a more subtle aberration. (1976, p. 396)

According to Cleckley, these are the main traits of psychopaths: superficial charm, adequate intelligence, absence of anxiety, insincerity, lack of remorse or shame, antisocial behavior, poor judgment, selfishness and egocentricity, lack of capacity for love, unemotional sexual behavior, lack of long-term life plans, and rarely, if ever, suicidal attempts.

Karpman (1948, 1959) introduced the distinction between primary, "idiopathic," that is, real psychopathy, and secondary, that is, merely "symptomatic" psychopathy. The secondary psychopathy includes antisocial and aggressive neurotics and psychotics. The genuine idiopathic, primary psychopaths have no conscience, no guilt feelings, and no generous emotions. They are usually motivated by selfish and uninhibited instinctive drives. Karpman further divided the primary psychopathy into two groups: (1) aggressive-predatory and (2) passive-parasitic. The aggressive-predatory type includes those who are entirely egoistic and have no compassion and no sympathetic feelings for anyone. They have no regard whatsoever for the rights of others, nor any concern for their feelings. The entire life of psychopaths is a life of aggressive predator animals. The passive-parasitic type has all the same traits common to all psychopaths except that they are not actively predatory; they prefer parasitic behavior; they attach themselves to other people and bleed them.

Karpman studied the dreams of the psychopaths. Their dream life has the characteristic pathognomonic structure and offers diagnostic clues. Most of their dreams are shallow with an immediate reaction to motor impulses. Anxiety dreams are rare, and they usually convey actual fear in the face of danger. There is a minimum of symbolism in psychopaths' dreams; the psychopaths usually dream of doing what they like to do or of obtaining what they want.

The psychopath's world is comprised of (1) himself or herself, (2) the "suckers," that is, all those who succumb to the psychopath's wishes, and (3) the "bastards," that is, those who refuse to comply with the psychopath's wishes.

10

Psychoanalysis and Related Systems

FREUDIAN VIEWS

Aichhorn (1935) described the lack of guilt feelings in juvenile delinquents and stressed the inadequate or missing superego. Aichhorn related antisocial behavior to the "defective ego ideal," that is, defective superego.

Aichhorn divided the delinquent adolescents into three groups. "Criminals from a sense of guilt" belonged to the first group; they practiced punishment-provoking antisocial behavior. Obviously they were not sociopaths but guilt-ridden neurotics who wished to be punished.

The second group was comprised of children and adolescents with a "nonsocial superego" created by identification with antisocial parental norms and values. "Primitive delinquents" who had very little or practically no superegos belonged to the third group. Apparently, the members of the second and third of Aichhorn's groups were sociopaths. The members of the second and third groups, the sociopaths, received in childhood no love and no affection, and most of them were brought up by aggressive and punitive parents. Aichhorn believed that the antisocial acting-out was related to Oedipal rebellion against the hostile father.

Anna Freud (1949) emphasized the role of early childhood

in the development of normal or antisocial personality. The newborn child is totally narcissistic, and it must gradually develop from the primary narcissism toward object love. A stable, caring, and affectionate parental attitude fosters the transition from a narcissistic cathexis of libido in oneself toward a gradual cathexis of libido in those who care for the child. An unstable or rejecting maternal attitude prevents the object-cathexis of the libido, and the child grows into a narcissistic, self-involved, selfish individual. Moreover, while his or her libido remains self-cathected, the lack of maternal love leaves the aggressive destrudo impulses unrestrained, and the sociopathic individual loves himself and is hostile to everyone else. In some cases the growth of the sociopathic antisocial personality is linked to pre-Oedipal and Oedipal conflicts with the rejecting and/or hostile parents. Unable to identify with the parents, the child grows without or with an exceedingly weak superego, unable to develop feelings of guilt or moral convictions.

Eissler (1949) related the origins of sociopathic personality to injustices experienced in early childhood. The unfair treatment in early childhood interferes with the normal process of identification with the child's parents or parental substitutes, prevents the formation of the superego, and unleashes aggressive antisocial impulses. Sociopathic individuals lack anxiety and guilt feelings, and their destructive behavior gives them a magic feeling of omnipotence.

Bowlby (1952) maintained that a prolonged separation from the mother is the main cause of the formation of antisocial personality. Children who grew up without a mother or whose mother was absent frequently and for long periods or who did not care for them turn to lying and stealing. Most of them become exceedingly selfish and develop antisocial, hostile attitudes typical for sociopaths.

Greenacre (1945) questioned the possibility of any human being lacking anxiety, conscience, or defensive self-restraints. According to Greenacre, psychopaths have not resolved the Oedipal conflict and they stay close to the mother, which prevents identification with the father. Adult psychopaths repeatedly reenact their childhood, especially the phallic phase with the unresolved Oedipus complex. The psychopaths introject their mother's guilt about them; they tend to take over this guilt and act in a self-contradictory manner. They both rebel against and succumb to it.

Glover (1960) has drawn a distinction between two types of psychopaths, namely, (1) the "private" and "benign" psychopathy, in which the condition affects the individual's "private life and character," and (2) the "malignant" or "criminal" psychopathy, where the disorder is demonstrated in "serious and persistent antisocial manifestations." Glover explained the benign psychopathy as follows:

> It is incidentally psychopathic personality. They do not see either a qualitative or quantitative deficiency in the social interactions of the individual. . . . no certain type of environment will cause the psychopathic personality, for psychopaths come from the most diverse types of environment and home conditions.

Bender (1947) noticed that the psychopathic personality traits appear quite early in one's life. Psychopathic children are impulsive, antisocial, and aggressive; they lack concern and consideration for others, do not experience guilt-feelings, and are unable to form friendship relations.

According to Schmideberg (1961), psychopathic personality is a product of disturbed object relations rather than of lack of superego. Schmideberg believes that "depersonalization" is a defense mechanism of the psychopaths. The development of adaptive ego functions is prevented by parental hostile attitudes; thus the normal attachments to parents or parental substitutes could not develop. Internalization and identification could not take place; thus the child who becomes a psychopath has no superego that could restrain the instinctual impulses and serve as a positive guide to socially acceptable behavior.

Levy (1951) distinguished between the "deprived" and the "indulged" psychopaths. The "deprived" psychopath is unable to adjust to life because he never experienced a close, personal relationship in infancy. As a consequence of the emotional deficit, he becomes unaffected by the need to be loved. The superego of the deprived psychopaths is very weak, and their ability to develop moral standards is defective, if it exists at all. The "indulged" psychopaths' mothers have never denied them anything. Their aggressiveness develops freely, and they become immune to punishment. The superego in the indulged psychopaths is weak because of their partial and inconsistent identification with the indulgent mothers.

According to Lippman (1959), rejected children tend to become psychopathic. Unwanted or rejected children of neurotic, sadistic, and ambivalent parents usually become very selfish, motivated by extreme narcissism and hostile feelings toward their parents and teachers. Lippman wrote: "It is the narcissism, resulting from rejection, which accounts for the inability of the child to form an object relation to his mother in the first year of life, to his father and siblings later and to those in the external world with whom he comes in contact" (p. 6).

In his study of the effect of early separation from the mother in shaping the personality of the psychopath, Spitz (1959) observed that the mother's unpredictable and rapidly changing attitudes prevent the establishment of object relations in the first year of life. This encourages narcissism and impairs the normal process of identification. In some cases, the identification with the mother becomes impossible because of the self-contradictory maternal attitudes. In other cases, the child who becomes a psychopath encounters several rapidly changing mother-substitutes, whose attitudes and personalities make them unpredictable and confusing to the child.

NON-FREUDIAN VIEWS

According to Sullivan (1953), a hostile mother causes an intense state of anxiety in the child. The hostile mother's attitude gravely affects the child's self-confidence. As the child gradually becomes aware of the "significant people," he or she learns to act in a manner that should help in gaining their approval. The child who experiences tenderness, approval, and good feelings develops a perception of oneself as "good me," whereas parental disapproval and rejection lead to perception of oneself as "bad me." A child acquires self-acceptance and self-respect if the significant people in his life have been affectionate and respectful to him.

When certain impulses cannot be openly expressed because they might elicit disapproval, the child may convey them in a camouflaged way and cover up his or her anxiety. Since sublimation may not be possible, the child may regress to an earlier developmental stage. Some children could undergo a malevolent transformation of personality in their craving for parental tenderness. Since the feelings of disapproval and the resulting anxiety lead to the formation of "bad me," the child may experience anxiety whenever the need for tenderness is frustrated. Sometimes the children conceal their anxiety by a hostile counterattacking of the rejecting parents. Feeling unceasingly endangered, the child refuses to risk experiencing the anxiety that becomes attached to any expression of tenderness.

Sullivan (1953, p. 124) maintains that the child learns that it is

> . . . highly disadvantageous to show any need for tender cooperation from authoritative figures about him, in which case he shows something else: and that something else is the basic malevolent attitude, the attitude that one really lives among enemies. . . . And on that basis . . . later in life . . . the juvenile makes it practically impossible for anyone to feel tenderly towards him.

Masterson (1980) has utilized Melanie Klein's version of psychoanalysis in treating juvenile delinquents. Borrowing Margaret Mahler's concept of separation-individuation, Masterson hypothesized that some delinquents failed in infancy to separate from the hostile and rejecting mother. The profound feeling of frustration leads to rage and depressive moods, and the child projects his or her own bad introject on the environment and attacks it. Thus, sociopathic behavior is a projection of hostile and revengeful attitudes to one's rejecting mother.

11

Learning Theories

Behavioral psychologists believe that antisocial behavior is acquired through the learning process of following the parental or any other role-model (Bandura, 1973). The parents of acting-out sociopaths set an example of verbal and physical abusive behavior, and their children are brought up in an environment that shapes the sociopath's behavior patterns. The sociopath rarely, if ever, had a peaceful dinner at home; usually father and mother traded verbal insults that occasionally led to physical violence. Both parents never missed the opportunity to hit the child, and corporal punishment occurred quite often.

Sociopaths are exceedingly sensitive to discomfort and pain. Some of them act out aggressively, sometimes in a self-destructive way, in order to avoid a difficult situation or unpleasant feeling. An adult patient of mine picked a fight with his superiors whenever he expected their disapproval for whatever mistakes he might have made. Needless to say, by this verbal aggression he caused more harm to his position. Agee (1979) noticed that aggressive behavior serves as an escape from facing a stressful situation or bad feelings; he called the sociopath an "aversive treatment evader." This aversive treatment evasion could be a product of experience and a result of the learning process.

Bandura et al. (1963) defined aggression as behavior aimed at inflicting injury on another person. Following the study by Dollard et al. (1939) on frustration and aggression, Bandura maintained that frustration leads to aggression, but the pattern of aggression depends on the individual's prior experiences. Moreover, Bandura and other learning theorists (Berkowitz, 1962; Ross, 1980) avoided Dollard's generalization and noticed that frustration could lead to various reactions and not always to aggression. The learning process is open to a variety of behavioral patterns: frustration may elicit anxiety, dependency, and also constructive efforts to remedy the situation and prevent future frustrations.

Bandura and Walters (1959) maintained that rage is the infant's earliest response to frustration. However, rage is not necessarily an aggressive and hostile reaction aimed at hurting someone; it is rather an impulsive reaction to pain or discomfort. Some children learn that they can hurt others, and the spontaneous screaming or kicking in a rage becomes transformed into intentional hostile acts aimed at forcing the parents and other people to give in to their wishes. Thus, aggressive behavior serves as an instrument for gaining concessions, and screaming and kicking and verbal or physical abuse become means for obtaining gratification. In some individuals aggressive behavior may become an important goal in itself, and they derive pleasure from hurting other people. Aggressive parents foster such a development, and sociopathic behavior patterns are learned by imitation and modeling.

It seems that the father's punitive actions, and especially corporal punishments, serve as a model for their children and encourage the process or learning of aggressive behavior. The fathers of aggressive boys do not tolerate any aggression directed to themselves; they usually counteract their sons' aggression in harsh and vehement manners. However, they are usually quite tolerant and even encouraging of their sons' physical aggressiveness directed against their peers. In other words, the boys are taught not to attack strong adversaries, but to take the liberty of assaulting weaker people, which is typical of sociopathic behavior. Some mothers of sociopathic children and/or adolescents are quite tolerant of their children's aggressiveness directed toward themselves, thus teaching them that aggression against weak people is permitted.

According to Bandura, imitation of and identification with the parent reflect the natural tendency of human beings "to match the behavior or attitudes as exhibited by actual or symbolic models" (1969, p. 215). In an experimental research study, subjects who watched a model who reacted aggressively to frustration tended to match and imitate the particular forms of aggression shown by the model (Bandura et al., 1963; Berkowitz, 1962), whether the model was an adult, a filmed adult, or a cartoon character.

There is plenty of evidence that children imitate the aggressive behavior of an adult model, even without reinforcers. Children tend to imitate an aggression that is rewarded more than an aggression that is not rewarded. Imitation of aggressive behavior can take place without direct reinforcement, but imitation is considerably facilitated by positive reinforcement.

The socialization process of children depends on direct conditioning and training, and it is encouraged and reinforced by identification with significant adults. Children tend to follow parental behavior which they observe and learn, even when parental behavior is not directly taught to them. For instance, when the parents administer physical punishment to a child for the child's aggressive behavior, the parents do not intend to increase the child's aggressiveness, but the punishment, acting as a frustration, increases the child's motivation for aggressive behavior, and the child is provided with an aggressive model of the physically punishing parent. Apparently, children tend to imitate aggressive adult models, and they learn through imitation of the aggressive behavior that the parents exhibit (Bandura et al., 1961).

Sears stresses the effects of punishment that provide the child with an aggressive model: "When the parents punish, particularly when they employ physical punishment, they are providing a living example of the use of aggression at the very moment they are trying to teach the child not to be aggressive. The child, who copies his parents in many ways, is likely to learn much from this example of successful aggression on the part of his parent" (Sears et al., 1957, p. 266). Sears maintains that punishment fosters an avoidance response while eliciting the wish to practice punishing action on others. The fear of punishment produces "aggression anxiety"; the child's antisocial behavior may be temporarily inhibited but not completely eliminated. The aggressive child who was punished for his or her aggressive behavior toward the parents may refrain from further aggression toward them. However, this same child might take out his or her aggression on another child or a pet animal.

12

Hyperinstrumental-Narcissistic Interpretation

There are three types of social interaction, namely, the "instrumental-taking" attitude, where one is concerned with satisfying one's own needs, the "mutual-give and take" attitude, and the "vectorial-giving" attitude. The child-parent attitude is instrumental, for the child needs all the support he or she can get. Mature adults interact in friendship and marriage on a give-and-take basis, and their interaction is mutual. Mature parents are ready to give to their children whatever they can without expecting anything in return, and they act in a vectorial-giving manner.

Serious distortions in the three normal types of social interaction lead to three types of mental disorders, namely, "hypervectorialism" in schizophrenia, "dysmutualism" in depressive disorders, and "hyperinstrumentalism" in sociopathy.

The hyperinstrumental is an emotionally primitive individual who has never outgrown the primary narcissism of infancy. The abnormal manifestation of depression is the core of the dysmutual personality disorder. The accepting-rejecting child-rearing practices make the child hate the parents for not giving love to him. The child blames oneself for not being loved by them and can never get enough love to make up for the rejection.

Certain intrafamilial relationships are even more detrimental to a child's personality. One of these is the *reversal of social roles*. When immature parents act as though they were the children, and they demand the kind of love and affection that would more properly be expected to come from their own parents, the child is forced into a costly, loving, hypervectorial attitude toward his parents.

As a result, the hypervectorials are unselfish, hyperethical, and self-righteous. They usually feel they are not as good as they ought to be and fear their own hostility. Schizophrenia is the name given to hypervectorialism in other diagnostic systems.

It seems that all three *types* of mental disorders could be related to both predisposing genetic and sociocultural factors. Many disorders can be understood as more or less severe manifestations of these three types. There are five levels of severity: (1) neurosis, (2) character neurosis, (3) latent psychosis, (4) manifest psychosis, and (5) dementia. Each step in these levels is characterized by successive failure of ego defenses and personality structure.

Neurosis, the first level of severity, is characterized by maintenance of ego defenses; *character neurosis* occurs when these ego defenses are blended into the personality; *latent psychosis* occurs when the ego controls begin to fail but some contact with reality is maintained; *manifest psychosis* occurs when the ego fails to maintain contact with reality; and *dementia* occurs when the personality structure collapses. (See Table 1.)

A hyperinstrumental treats people as if they were tools to be used or food to be eaten. He is not friendly to strong and friendly individuals or to strong and hostile ones; he himself could never be friendly toward weak ones, and friendliness on the part of the strong ones makes him suspicious. Hyperinstrumentals do not believe that anyone can be genuinely friendly, honest, or self-sacrificing. They are convinced that the world is a jungle and they must look out for themselves.

TABLE 1
Classification of Mental Disorders

Level	Hyperinstrumental-Narcissistic Disorders	Dysmutual Disorders	Hypervectorial-Schizotype Disorders
Neurotic	Hyperinstrumental neurosis (certain anxiety and inferiority reactions)	Depressive neurosis (dissociation hysterias)	Hypervectorial neurosis (obsessional, phobic, and neurasthenic neuroses)
Character neurosis	Hyperinstrumental character neurosis (sociopathic personality)	Depressive character neurosis (cyclothymic and passive aggressive personality)	Hypervectorial character neurosis (schizoid and compulsive personality)
Latent psychosis	Latent hyperinstrumental psychosis (sociopathic reactions bordering on psychosis)	Latent depressive psychosis (borderline manic-depressive psychosis)	Latent hypervectorial psychosis (borderline and latent schizophrenia)
Manifest psychosis	Hyperinstrumental psychosis	Depressive psychosis	Vectoriasis praecox (manifest schizophrenia)
Dementia	Collapse of personality structure		

ANTISOCIAL BEHAVIOR

Not all antisocial behavior is a product of the instrumental-narcissistic personality structure and its peculiar dysbalance of libido and destrudo cathexes. Antisocial and aggressive behavior can be caused by a variety of organic, social, and psychological factors. The present volume does not deal with brain injuries, tumors, epilepsies, and the organic mental disorders; it must, however, be clearly stated that antisocial and violent behavior can be produced by organic causes as well.

Hostility is not limited to the narcissistic-instrumental type.

Hostile behavior, which is a given of human nature, starts with the object-directed destrudo in infancy. From a phylogenetic and ontogenetic point of view, hostility begins prior to the development of object-directed libido and represents the fundamental method of struggle for survival. There are, however, distinct developmental stages in the cathexes of libido and destrudo.

Adjustment to one's society is one of the most important determinants of mental health. No society can tolerate unrestricted aggression, and civilized cultures permit the use of force in self-defense only, and only in a way prescribed by their respective legal systems. Well-adjusted individuals keep their hostile impulses under control imposed by the ego and superego. Whether they compete or cooperate, love or hate, they are not carried away by their impulses. Neither saints nor sinners, they act reasonably, in instrumental, mutual, and vectorial ways depending on the circumstances. They are not afraid to bear hostility against those who hurt them; in such situations they defend their rights within socially approved limits.

Infantile hostility is as irrational as the hostile behavior of mentally disturbed individuals. The three types of mental disorders display three distinct patterns of hostile feelings and actions. The schizoid-hypervectorial's hostile behavior is primarily inspired by the superego and directed against guilt feelings motivated by a true or imaginary failure to give love and support to parents or parental figures. When the ego-protective defense mechanisms fail, the self-directed hatred pours out against anyone in indiscriminate violence. The depressive-dysmutual hates those who do not love him and hates himself for not being loved. The sociopathic-hyperinstrumental does not criticize himself for hating other people and is concerned with satisfaction of own needs with no concern for anyone else. The hostile feelings of the sociopaths are primitive, infantile, and directed against whoever does not succumb to their wishes. In milder forms of sociopathy, the ego exercises some degree of self-control in fear of retaliation; severely disturbed hyperinstrumentals are unable to control their sexual and aggressive impulses and become a menace to society. Driven by the id-governed pleasure principle, they demand immediate gratification at the expense of other people, and they tend to act impulsively.

Sociopaths are unable to tolerate pain, discomfort, or frustration and have little, if any, sense of responsibility. Most of them lack insight and are unable to accept blame, to feel guilty, or to have concern for anyone but themselves.

In several cases the mothers of sociopaths are severely disturbed individuals unable to take care of their children. In many instances the sociopathic child is exploited and ridiculed by the father and the mother. Sociopaths are never proud of their parents, and tender feelings toward their parents are virtually nonexistent. Parental neglect and/or misguided hyperpermissiveness often contributes to sociopathy in the offspring.

Hyperinstrumentals believe that they are poor, innocent, hungry, lonely, and mistreated creatures. Whether or not a hyperinstrumental-sociopath will become an overt criminal depends largely on circumstances. He is a criminal at heart who will or will not commit a crime depending on the weakness of his victim and the danger involved in attack. Most hyperinstrumentals avoid antisocial acts for which they might be punished; when they are caught, they regret not the crime but the punishment. They are Eichmanns, not Raskolnikovs.

The outstanding trait of the hyperinstrumental is his extreme narcissism. The hyperinstrumental sociopaths are concerned neither with giving nor with receiving love. They want food, whether it is given with or without love; they want sex, with or without affection; what they want most are material possessions, comforts, and power.

One may distinguish between "aggressive-sadistic" and "parasitic-exploitative" sociopaths. A "parasitic-exploitative" sociopath does not rape a woman when there are people nearby. He may, however, become less cautious and more impulsive and may attack, rape, or torture a lonely girl, an aging woman, or a cripple. "Moral insanity" is indeed the right name for the "aggressive-sadistic" sociopath who ripped away the abdomen of one woman and bit off a part of another woman's breast.

Fear is perhaps the only contact with reality in aggressive-sadistic sociopaths who fear policemen only when they see them alert and well-armed. Aggressive-sadistic sociopaths display poor judgment, inadequate perception of reality, and no understanding of the potential consequences of their deeds. They often torture their victims and derive pleasure from inflicting pain. They usually rob their victims, although robbery itself does not give them adequate pleasure. Additional pleasure will be gained from beating, stabbing, and other forms of violence.

The parasitic-exploitative sociopaths avoid work and, whenever possible, live a parasitic life. They try to escape legitimate employment; many of them become racketeers, extortionists, and nonviolent criminals. When they deteriorate, they become drunkards and addicts, beggars, and bums.

The Nazis were aggressive-sadistic sociopaths. The Russian writer Ilya Ehrenburg told the following story about German prisoners of World War II: When asked whether their invasion of Poland, Holland, Belgium, Denmark, Norway, and France was right, they said that all the invasions were justified. They admitted, however, that the invasion of Russia was morally wrong, because in this instance Germany had failed. World War I was not a blunder, but a betrayal: the moderate Treaty of Versailles was an injustice perpetrated on the poor Germans who deserved to conquer the world and turn it into one huge concentration camp.

The Nazi mentality was clearly sociopathic. The guards of concentration camps felt pity for their pet animals, but had nothing but contempt for their victims. Some Nazi guards took pleasure in murdering men, women, and children while listening to sentimental music.

DESTRUDO

The hyperinstrumental's use of violence is not only for tangible gains. His deeply rooted inferiority feelings motivate him to hurt others, not only for money or other gains, but also for a show of power. Hyperinstrumentals may kill even after they have robbed the victim; they often torture and mutilate in robbery and rape, because cruelty enhances their feeling of power.

They do not experience genuine feelings of guilt. They experience neither regret nor self-accusation on moral grounds, though they hate themselves for being weak or for not being shrewd enough to escape punishment. Feelings of depression in hyperinstrumentals can originate in a loss of support or loss of property, failure in business or school, loss of a job, fear, feelings of weakness and inadequacy in the face of danger, inability to cope with a job, failure to escape penalty, and so on. It is usually a combination of destructive impulses directed toward others. A hyperinstrumental hates the world that refuses to satisfy his needs and blames it for his frustrations. The hyperinstrumental, convinced of his innocence, rarely, if ever, feels that he deserves punishment.

SEX

Most hyperinstrumentals remain fixated on infantile sexual levels. They are guided by a desire to avoid disapproval; fear is the only inhibitory factor that prevents sociopaths from acting out their impulses. The pleasure principle, that is, the principle of immediate gratification of needs, is the main motive in the life of sociopaths.

A 40-year-old male patient practiced sex with animals, children, men, women, whatever sex objects were available. He knew society condemned his behavior, but he himself did not feel that he was wrong. His only fear was of being caught; thus he neither raped nor killed. He did maintain, however, that if he could get away with murder, "he certainly would commit it."

A sociopathic woman, married, 28 years old, was having, as she put it, "occasional" affairs with men. "As long as my husband did not know," she said, "he was not hurt."

SUPEREGO AND MORALITY

An inadequate development of the superego is usually a result of inadequate or totally missing opportunity for identifying oneself with parental figures. A patient of mine was brought up in an institution that preached religious devotion while practicing the laws of the jungle. Because they had kitchen chores, the children were in a position to compare their own strictly rationed and meager food with the luxurious meals of their educators. Shortage of food and lack of educational guidance led to a general practice of thievery; whenever a child did not appear on time at his table, his or her food was stolen by other children.

The children wore shabby clothes all year round with the exception of days when important visitors were expected; then clean bedspreads, neat tablecloths, and special "holiday" clothes were distributed. The counselors frequently took monetary and sexual advantage of the children, who did not dare to complain because of fear of punishments.

A sociopathic child may identify with the strong aggressor and develop a crude and pathological superego. A young patient identified with the "smart tough guys" who knew how to take advantage of other people, but could not identify with his middle-class parents who were unable to provide any guidance whatsoever. This patient tried to abstain from violence because of its dangerous implications, but he would not refrain from cheating, theft, drinking, and sexual license.

A sociopath can easily become a criminal, although he is less likely to do so if the norms and laws in his society are strict and violation of the law invites social ostracism and severe punishment. Thus, many sociopaths lead the lives of honest citizens, not out of integrity but because it is most advantageous to be socially accepted.

HYPERINSTRUMENTAL (SOCIOPATHIC) NEUROSIS

Sociopaths on the neurotic level are selfish, dishonest, exploitative individuals who feel cheated and exploited by others. They resent the fact that the world is not as nice to them as they would like it to be. Most of them are continuously dissatisfied; they doubt their own abilities, feel insecure and threatened, and develop a great variety of mental and psychosomatic symptoms. The sociopathic neurotic alleviates his feelings of inadequacy and gains privileges through his pathological symptoms. The sole reason for a sociopath's self-control is fear that acting out his hostile impulses will invite retaliation and he will be hurt. The world is seen by sociopathic neurotics as a hostile place, and all of them see the world in a paranoid manner.

HYPERINSTRUMENTAL CHARACTER NEUROSIS

Hyperinstrumental character neurosis reflects, as do all other character neuroses, the acceptance of neurotic symptoms as a protective shell. As is true of other character neurotics, the hyperinstrumentals glorify their shortcomings and mistake faults for virtues. In the hyperinstrumental character neurosis, the gains are immediate and tangible, and neurotic symptoms are designed to procure definite benefits. One patient used psychosomatic symptoms to be excused from household chores; another exploited his alleged physical illness for gaining food privileges at home; another female patient obtained concessions from her co-workers in terms of working hours and efficiency, expecting consideration and special privileges because she told them that she was a "disturbed person."

LATENT HYPERINSTRUMENTAL PSYCHOSIS

Latent psychotic sociopaths are frequently aware of their murderous impulses and fear they may lose control and be severely punished. Latent psychotic hyperinstrumentals are humorless, irritable, quarrelsome, hostile, greedy, and suspicious. They are either overtly hostile or passive and apathetic, regressing into a parasitic pattern of vegetation. "I am either a tiger or a vegetable," said a latent psychotic hyperinstrumental.

Latent psychotic sociopaths are realistic enough to fear being caught while they rape or practice exhibitionism, sadism, or homosexuality. They will often develop paranoid fears and suspect that they are being watched or persecuted. Their paranoid delusions are less persistent than those of hypervectorials and less elaborate and systematized than the paranoid delusions of the dysmutuals.

The weak inhibitions and self-control of hyperinstrumental latent psychotics fail under the impact of anger, sexual urge, alcohol, disappointment, or fatigue. As is the case with latent psychotics of the two other types (hypervectorial and dysmutual), latent psychotic hyperinstrumentals live on the edge of a volcano that may erupt at the slightest provocation.

MANIFEST SOCIOPATHIC PSYCHOSIS

A manifest hyperinstrumental psychotic has no aims, no plans, no goals, no aspirations, no ideals, no clear conception of reality, no self-control. Blindly following his needs, whims, and impulses, he seeks an immediate gratification of his wishes with no consideration for future consequences.

DEMENTIVE LEVEL

Dementive sociopathic psychotics usually end up in jails and/or in mental hospitals. Sociopathic dementia is a state of deep regression to subhuman life. Dementive hyperinstrumentals feel sorry for themselves and resent "unfair treatment" in jail, but they have no sympathy for anyone else. Their mental horizons shrink to the most primitive functions; their perceptive functions are severely disturbed and their memory is practically nonexistent.

Subhuman standards are most characteristic of dementive hyperinstrumentals. They are concerned only with food, elimination, sleep, and sex. They have no shame, no faith, no inhibitions, no civilization. Hyperinstrumental psychotics cannot perceive, think, or reason; their personality has been reduced to their stomach and intestines, bowels and bladder, penis or vagina.

Their minds stop existing; their ego and superego fall apart; what is left is just an animalistic id.

PART IV

Diagnostic and Treatment Methods

13

Diagnosing Sociopathic Personality

DIAGNOSTIC PROBLEMS

Dissimilar causes can produce similar results. To put it more precisely, a cluster A B C and a cluster D E F are quite different; they may, however, produce very similar symptoms. For instance, severe anxiety can be caused by physical injuries such as a common cold, dyspepsia, a broken limb, and any other physical injury. Anxiety can also be caused by a threat of loss of a job, by rejection from a parent or a lover, by death in the family, or by any other personal misfortune, as well as by a war or an earthquake. Different causes can produce similar results, making the diagnostic task quite difficult.

Ultimately, diagnostic work is an exercise in formal logic. Aspiring clinicians, psychiatrists, psychologists, and neurologists should receive adequate training in logic, for logic can be of great help in diagnosing patients. Take, for instance, depression. There are many negative and unpleasant emotional reactions such as disappointment, frustration, insecurity, inferiority, guilt, remorse, anxiety, mourning, and so on. There is, however, one specific clinical entity of depression comprised of self-directed blame and anger. Depressed individuals blame themselves for being weak, helpless creatures and hate themselves for being this way.

Let us take another example of diagnostic difficulties, for instance: schizophrenia. The name itself, coined 80 years ago by E. Bleuler, is a misnomer, for there is nothing particularly "split" in the minds of schizophrenics. However, certain frequent symptoms, such as delusions, hallucinations, withdrawal, self-righteousness, and belligerence, are not exclusively schizophrenic traits; thus they cannot serve as totally dependable criteria for differential diagnosis.

Typical sociopathic behavioral patterns can be observed in a variety of neurological disorders, such as encephalitis lethargica. Many postencephalitic patients are extremely selfish, act in an antisocial and aggressive manner, lie, and steal. In their antisocial behavior they closely resemble the sociopaths' behavior; however, their antisocial behavior does not allow including them in the clinical category of sociopathic personality.

A few years ago I came across a middle-aged, well-mannered, and highly ethical business executive. After suffering a brain injury, he turned into an antisocial, shameless, violent, and cruel individual. He lost all control over his behavior; whenever his wife and child did not follow his whims, he cursed them and physically attacked them. He has become extremely selfish, impulsive, irresponsible, exploitative, and belligerent, in short, a typical sociopath. However, prior to the brain injury, he was a friendly and considerate individual, a loving husband and a caring father.

Many years ago when I was director of a sleep-in institution for disturbed children and adolescents, I had a few epileptics there. Their behavior frequently resembled that of sociopaths; they were inconsiderate, selfish, impulsive, manipulative, and occasionally violent. However, they were not consistently sociopathic; quite often their behavior resembled obsessive-compulsive neurosis.

Children with minimal brain dysfunction have little concern for others, tend to lie, steal, and be verbally and physically abusive. A 16-year-old boy I saw for consultation was sent away for one year to a correctional institution where he conformed perfectly to the rules and regulations. When he regained his freedom and returned home, he went back to his antisocial, selfish, and exploitative behavior with frequent violent outbursts.

DIAGNOSTIC CRITERIA OF THE AMERICAN PSYCHIATRIC ASSOCIATION

In 1957 the Committee on Public Information of the American Psychiatric Association defined a psychopath as "a person whose behavior is predominantly amoral or antisocial and characterized by impulsive, irresponsible actions satisfying only immediate and narcissistic interests without concern for obvious and implicit social consequences accompanied by minimal outward evidence of anxiety or guilt."

The *Diagnostic and Statistical Manual of Mental Disorders* of the American Psychiatric Association (DSM-III, 1980) offers the following diagnostic clues for narcissistic personality disorder and antisocial personality disorder:

> The following are characteristic of the individual's current and long-term functioning, are not limited to episodes of illness, and cause either significant impairment in social or occupational functioning or subjective distress:
> A. Grandiose sense of self-importance or uniqueness, e.g., exaggeration of achievements and talents, focus on the special nature of one's problems.
> B. Preoccupation with fantasies of unlimited success, power, brilliance, beauty or ideal love.
> C. Exhibitionism: the person requires constant attention and admiration.
> D. Cool indifference or marked feelings of rage, inferiority, shame, humiliation, or emptiness in response to criticism, indifference of others, or defeat.
> E. At least two of the following characteristic of disturbances in interpersonal relationships:
>   1) entitlement: expectation of special favors without assuming reciprocal responsibilities, e.g., surprise and anger that people will not do what is wanted

2) interpersonal exploitativeness: taking advantage of others to indulge own desires or for self-aggrandizement; disregard for the personal integrity and rights of others
3) relationships that characteristically alternate between the extremes of overidealization and devaluation
4) lack of empathy: inability to recognize how others feel, e.g., unable to appreciate the distress of someone who is seriously ill. . . .

Differential Diagnosis: Conduct Disorder consists of the typical childhood signs of Antisocial Personality Disorder. Since such behavior may terminate spontaneously or evolve into other disorders such as Schizophrenia, a diagnosis of Antisocial Personality Disorder should not be made in children; it is reserved for adults (18 or over) who have had time to show the full longitudinal pattern.

Adult Antisocial Behavior, in the category Conditions Not Attributable to a Mental Disorder, should be considered when the criminal or other aggressive or antisocial behavior occurs in individuals who do not meet the full criteria for Antisocial Personality Disorder and whose antisocial behavior cannot be attributed to any other mental disorder.

When *Substance Abuse* and antisocial behavior begin in childhood and continue into adult life, both Substance Use Disorder and Antisocial Personality Disorder should be diagnosed if the criteria for each disorder are met, regardless of the extent to which some of the antisocial behavior may be a consequence of the Substance Use Disorder, e.g., illegal selling of drugs, or the assaultive behavior associated with Alcohol Intoxication. When antisocial behavior in an adult is associated with a Substance Use Disorder, the diagnosis of Antisocial Personality is not made unless the childhood signs of Antisocial Personality Disorder were also present and continued without a remission of five years or more between age 15 and adult life.

Severe Mental Retardation and Schizophrenia preempt the diagnosis of Antisocial Personality Disorder, because at the present time there is no way to determine when antisocial behavior that occurs in an individual with severe Mental Retardation or Schizophrenia is due to these more severe disorders or to Antisocial Personality Disorder.

Manic episodes may be associated with antisocial behavior.

The differential diagnosis is easily made by noting the absence of severe behavior problems in childhood and the sudden change in adult behavior. (DSM-III, pp. 317–319)

SOME DIAGNOSTIC METHODS

Several diagnostic methods have been used with various degrees of success. The Rorschach Inkblot Test was applied by some research workers who studied impulsive and/or antisocial behavior. Crain and Smoke (1981) tested agressiveness in children. The most aggressive children gave most "victim" responses, apparently perceiving themselves as innocent victims of a hostile environment, typical for sociopaths whom I called "innocent criminals" (Wolman, 1973).

Kempler and Scott (1970) applied the Thematic Apperception Test in a study of adolescents. The stories of antisocial, aggressive adolescents reflected lack of interpersonal relationships, lack of concern for anyone except themselves, plenty of hostile feelings, and very little, if any, guilt feelings.

Hathaway and Monachesi tested in the late 1940s 4,000 ninth-grade students with the Minnesota Multiphasic Personality Inventory (MMPI). They conducted follow-up studies in 1950 and 1952 when their subjects were about 17 years old. A high score on the Psychopathic Deviate scale was associated with a high rate of delinquency (1953).

Further studies conducted with the MMPI found a connection between the T scores on scale 4 (Psychopathic Deviate) and juvenile delinquency (Huesmann et al., 1978; Eron, 1980).

Graham (1978, p. 316) suggested MMPI criteria for differential diagnosis (see Table 2).

BEHAVIORAL CRITERIA

Robins (1977) suggested the following behavioral criteria for sociopathy, namely, difficulties in school, running away from home, early sexual problems, early alcoholism, per-

TABLE 2
Sample Interpretive Inferences for Standard MMPI Scales

Scale Name	Scale Abbreviation	Scale No.	Interpretation of High Scores	Interpretation of Low Scores
	L		Trying to create favorable impression by not being honest in responding to items; conventional; rigid; moralistic; lacks insight	Responded frankly to items; confident; perceptive; self-reliant; cynical
	F		May indicate invalid profile; severe pathology; moody; restless; dissatisfied	Socially conforming; free of disabling psychopathology; may be "faking good"
	K		May indicate invalid profile; defensive; inhibited; intolerant; lacks insight	May indicate invalid profile; exaggerates problems; self-critical; dissatisfied; conforming; lacks insight; cynical
Hypochondriasis	Hs	1	Excessive bodily concern; somatic symptoms; narcissistic; pessimistic; demanding; critical; long-standing problems	Free of somatic preoccupation; optimistic; sensitive; insightful
Depression	D	2	Depressed; pessimistic; irritable; dissatisfied; lacks self-confidence; introverted; overcontrolled	Free of psychological turmoil; optimistic; energetic; competitive; impulsive; undercontrolled; exhibitionistic

Hysteria	Hy	3	Physical symptoms of functional origin; lacks insight; self-centered; socially involved; demands attention and affection	Constricted; conventional narrow interests; limited social participation; untrusting; hard to get to know; realistic
Psychopathic Deviate	Pd	4	Asocial or antisocial; rebellious; impulsive; poor judgment; immature; creates good first impression; superficial relationships; aggressive; free of psychological turmoil	Conventional; conforming; accepts authority; low drive level; concerned about status and security; persistent; moralistic
Masculinity-femininity	Mf	5	Male: aesthetic interests; insecure in masculine role; creative; good judgment; sensitive; passive; dependent; good self-control Female: rejects traditional female role; masculine interests; assertive; competitive; self-confident; logical; unemotional	Male: overemphasized strength and physical prowess; adventurous; narrow interests; inflexible; contented; lacks insight Female: accepts traditional female role; passive; yielding to males; complaining; critical; constricted
Paranoia	Pa	6	May exhibit frankly psychotic behavior; suspicious; sensitive; resentful; projects; rationalizes; moralistic; rigid	May have frankly psychotic symptoms; evasive; defensive; guarded; secretive; withdrawn

TABLE 2 (Continued)
Sample Interpretive Inferences for Standard MMPI Scales

Scale Name	Scale Abbreviation	Scale No.	Interpretation of High Scores	Interpretation of Low Scores
Psychasthenia	Pt	7	Anxious; worried; difficulties in concentrating; ruminative; obsessive; compulsive; insecure; lacks self-confidence; organized; persistent; problems in decision making	Free of disabling fears and anxieties; self-confident; responsible; adaptable; values success and status
Schizophrenia	SC	8	May have thinking disturbance; withdrawn; self-doubts; feels alienated and unaccepted; vague goals	Friendly; sensitive, trustful; avoids deep emotional involvement; conventional; unimaginative
Hypomania	Ma	9	Excessive activity; impulsive; lacks direction; unrealistic self-appraisal; low frustration tolerance; friendly; manipulative; episodes of depression	Low energy level; apathetic; responsible; conventional; lacks self-confidence; overcontrolled
Social introversion	Si	0	Socially introverted; shy; sensitive; overcontrolled; conforming; problems in decision making	Socially extroverted; friendly; active; competitive; impulsive; self-indulgent

sistent lying, and trouble with police. Robins maintains that before they reach the age of 15, sociopaths have at least three of these symptoms, and after 15, they have at least two more, frequently related to job difficulties and marital discord. The antisocial symptoms in school include truancy and physical fighting with schoolmates, teachers, and administrators. The most frequent symptoms at the age of 18 and older include temper tantrums, physical violence, being fired from a job or quitting because of conflicts, and marital infidelity. Alcoholism, drug dependence, and crimes such as robbery, burglary, rape, and murder should be added to the list of behavioral diagnostic clues.

A detailed observational method of differential diagnosis was introduced by Wolman in his Sociodiagnostic Interview (Wolman, 1978). This method uses the terms hyperinstrumental for sociopaths, hypervectorial for schizoids and schizophrenics, and dysmutual for depressives.

Behavioral Clues

The diagnostic clues described below are not precise, rigid patterns but descriptive hints not to be taken literally. They are meaningful only in the context of a total personality picture.

1) Observations in terms of power may start with a general activity and vitality. Hypervectorials (schizophrenic type) display as a rule less vitality, less energy, and an overall reduced initiative and activity as compared to average normal subjects. They are more precise and pay more attention to detail but are usually much slower than other people. The hyperinstrumentals (sociopathic type) are active whenever it serves the satisfaction of their needs; otherwise they do not make much effort. The dysmutuals (manic-depressive type) are either senselessly hyperactive, doing things no one needs and being loud, verbose, and full of energy, or senselessly passive even when passivity jeopardizes their well-being.

2) In intellectual functioning the hypervectorials display

certain peculiarities. While they may be especially keen, attentive, and alert in one area, they often display lack of interest and apathy in many others. When involved in something, they are exceptionally perceptive, and their judgment is sharp and logical. The hyperinstrumentals seldom show such an acuity of mind; rarely are they seriously involved in anything outside their own immediate, usually material or sexual needs. The dysmutuals can be exceedingly alert at one moment and entirely oblivious at another.

3) The three types differ also in their patterns of thinking. Intelligence is not correlated with mental disorder, and one may find mental disorders associated with any degree of innate intellectual ability; there are intellectually inferior and superior individuals in all three types (Wolman, 1985). Certain peculiarities in the thought process are distinguishable by psychological tests and, in extreme cases, even in a simple observation. The hypervectorials tend to overlook real facts; they are logical (unless deteriorated) but not empirically minded. They are prone to indulge in abstract thinking and deep speculation with little regard for reality and overemphasis on minute detail. Their fantasy is rich but often unrealistic, leading to autistic thinking and bizarre reasoning.

Gifted sociopaths are more often plagiarists rather than inventors. Their thinking lacks depth, and their ideas are narrow. The dysmutuals are rarely as shrewd as hyperinstrumentals or as deep as hypervectorials; they are, as a rule, more practical than the hypervectorials and more profound than the hyperinstrumentals. When deteriorated, their mind goes blank and dull as in the hyperinstrumentals, that is, sociopaths.

4) The three types differ also in the intake of food. Food is highly important to hyperinstrumentals, who can barely stand any food deprivation. Hypervectorials are usually finicky eaters; eating is a problem to many schizophrenics. They either refuse to eat or overeat (to reduce anxiety) or toy with food. Dysmutuals eat quickly and often overeat. At meals in the hospital, schizophrenics are usually the slowest and manic-depressives are the fastest eaters.

5) The rhythm of waking and sleeping states is frequently disturbed in hypervectorials. Whenever disturbed, they have difficulties in falling asleep and cannot sleep the night through. On the neurotic level, sleep difficulties are often the outstanding symptom that brings the patient to the consultation room. In latent and manifest schizophrenics sleep disorders may become tantamount to the inability to fall asleep.

The hyperinstrumentals sleep well and like to sleep many hours, unless under threat. Dysmutuals either fall asleep whenever perturbed by either inner or outer threats or are unable to sleep when excited. In manifest, manic-depressive psychosis, they frequently go to bed early, being unable to stay up late in the evening. In depressive moods they wake up very early in the morning hating themselves and the world; in early hours the danger of suicide is quite high.

6) Personal care offers another clue in differential diagnosis. Hypervectorials do not care much for themselves but worry what other people will think about them. On the neurotic, character neurotic, and latent psychotic levels they are meticulously neat. Neglect in personal cleanliness and appearance is usually a sign of serious deterioration. On manifest and, even more, on dementive levels, all personal care may disappear entirely.

7) There are definite differences between the three types with regard to property and money. Hyperinstrumentals are greedy and acquisitive, hypervectorials are frugal, dysmutuals are inconsistent. Hyperinstrumentals grab what they can and are unwilling to share. Hypervectorials cannot part with their possessions and would rather spend money on others than on themselves.

8) Hyperinstrumentals are inclined to work hard only when driven by fear or reward; they cheat whenever they can. Hypervectorials are, as a rule, highly conscientious workers. Dysmutuals depend on their fluctuating moods.

9) In success, hypervectorials tend to worry; in failure, they blame themselves. Hyperinstrumentals in success act victorious, greedy, and triumphant; in defeat they become

subservient. Dysmutuals exaggerate in joyful self-praise at a slight success and exaggerate in blaming themselves and others whenever defeated.

10) With regard to pain, one can say that hypervectorials are masochistically inclined, hyperinstrumentals sadistically, and dysmutuals sadomasochistically. Hypervectorials frequently neglect their own health, notwithstanding pain. Hyperinstrumentals are highly sensitive to pain and overdo in demanding medical care. Dysmutuals go from one extreme to the other.

11) Hypervectorial schizo-type individuals fear their own hostile impulses that could prove to the world how bad they are. Hyperinstrumental sociopaths distrust and fear people. Dysmutuals in elation have no fear; in depression they fear everything.

12) Self-esteem is usually low in all three types. Feelings of inadequacy and dissatisfaction with oneself accompany all mental disorders. The hypervectorials feel most dissatisfied with themselves because they believe they are bad; they perceive themselves as hostile and worry lest others may feel the same way and blame them. The hyperinstrumentals worry about their own power only—the power to get what they need and destroy whatever is in their way. As one psychopathic patient put it, "I feel either like a tiger that can tear the world apart or like a vegetable, anyone can step over me." Their self-esteem depends on tangible achievements.

Manic-depressives combine the power and acceptance dimensions. They swing in their own eyes, from giants to dwarfs. When they feel accepted, they feel strong and friendly; when rejected, they feel weak and hostile to themselves and the outer world. Self-esteem in hypervectorials depends on whether their love has been accepted, that is, whether parental figures or another significant person whom they love has accepted their love. Dysmutuals need to receive love from everywhere and are never satiated; occasionally they may believe they are loved and enjoy short periods of elation.

INTERACTIONAL CLUES

There are distinct differences in the way the three types relate to and interact with other people.

1) Hypervectorials display a great deal of empathy; i.e., they sense the feelings of others. Instrumentals have very little empathy, if any. Dysmutuals have less empathy than hypervectorials and more than hyperinstrumentals. Schizophrenics are not always friendly, but they are usually understanding; sociopaths do not care about others; manic-depressives go from one extreme to the other.

2) Hypervectorials excel also in sympathy. Hyperinstrumentals have no sympathy and no mercy, but they expect sympathy from others. Dysmutuals go to extremes; occasionally they are hypersympathetic and self-sacrificing and swing back to an almost psychopathic cruelty. Hypervectorials are cruel when furious, back to an almost psychopathic cruelty. Hypervectorials are cruel when hurt; hyperinstrumentals are cruel when it pays to be; dysmutuals are cruel when agitated.

3) Hypervectorials in neurotic, latent psychotic, and remissive phases are usually tactful and considerate; they are often cold and cruel in schizotype character toward those they perceive as strong and tactless and brutal toward those they perceive as weak. Dysmutuals are oversentimental toward those whose love they wish to get and brutal toward those they do not care for; they are rarely tactful.

4) Moral rigidity characterizes hypervectorials; lack of morality is typical of hyperinstrumentals; moral inconsistency is the sign of dysmutualism. Hypervectorials cling to principles, are dogmatic and self-righteous. Hyperinstrumentals have no moral principles whatsoever; they are radical opportunists. Dysmutuals are idealistic and moralistic in one situation and the reverse in another. Hypervectorial schizotype individuals try hard to be godlike angels and fear that they are devils; when defenses fail, their destrudo erupts in a wild violence. Hyperinstrumentals are overtly selfish and always believe that they are within their rights. The whole

world seems to be one *Lebensraum* for their ever-hungry wolf jaws, while they believe themselves to be innocent sheep. Dysmutuals are Dr. Jekyll and Mr. Hyde; when they feel rejected, they become hostile and aggressive.

5) All disturbed individuals are prone to tell lies. Hyperinstrumentals lie whenever it is profitable. Hypervectorials rarely lie but may do so if their self-esteem is in jeopardy; they lie when they are afraid people will think they are bad or stupid. Dysmutuals lie frequently, usually for self-aggrandizement. Their lies are fantastic, often nonsensical; sometimes they say things that do not make sense even to themselves. Dysmutuals often sound insincere even when they are sincere.

6) The picture that hypervectorials have of other people is highly confused. They usually perceive others as better, stronger, smarter than themselves and the members of their family. Their feeling of inferiority spreads to those for whom they feel responsible.

Hyperinstrumentals divide the world into those to fear and those to exploit. Dysmutuals divide the world into those who love and those who reject.

7) Hypervectorials are slow to form friendship, but tend to get lastingly overinvolved and are unable to break off an attachment. Hyperinstrumentals have no friends on a give-and-take basis; a friend to them is someone to be exploited. Their friendships are formed for practical reasons and accordingly are either dropped or conveniently preserved. Dysmutuals easily develop profound attachments, but their feelings are rarely lasting.

8) Hypervectorials are quite persistent in love. When their love is not accepted, it turns into hate. Dysmutuals are never deeply in love, but they hate those who refuse to give love to them. Dysmutuals are "love addicts," constantly in search of new love objects. Their love is always ambivalent, and when it is not returned, it becomes hate. Hyperinstrumentals love no one except themselves.

9) Sexual deviations accompany all mental disorders. Sociopaths are most frequently polymorphous perverts, capable

of and willing to participate in any type of sexual activity. Schizophrenics are frequently torn by the conflict of sex identification and fear of homosexuality. Manic-depressives frequently display impotence, frigidity, and other sexual disturbances.

10) Hypervectorials try to control hostility; they display hostility whenever rejected, offended, or unable to bear inner hostility and when their defense mechanisms fail. Hyperinstrumentals are hostile whenever their needs are frustrated, that is, whenever their victims protest or anyone gets in their way. Dysmutual sociopaths frequently show ambivalent hostility, hating friends who do not love them enough. The schizophrenic fights because he cannot control hostile impulses; the sociopath fights to win; the manic-depressive vents his hostility whenever he is not loved. While hypervectorial schizophrenics are often hostile, they cannot take hostility; blame or criticism sets off hostile reactions in hypervectorials. Hyperinstrumentals will accept criticism from those they perceive as strong and retaliate for criticism coming from weak individuals. Dysmutuals are not very sensitive to criticism coming from strangers but become aggressive-depressive (i.e., hostile toward others and themselves) when criticized by those who are expected to love them.

In deep regression, hyperinstrumental sociopaths wish to bite and regress to cruelty and ruthless murder. Dysmutual manic-depressives wish to sleep and regress into a sleepy intrauterine, parasitic life. Hypervectorial schizophrenics do not wish anything; they withdraw from life, and if not taken care of, they will die.

Similar diagnostic clues can be obtained from the Psychosociodiagnostic Interview. The main difference between the Interview and the Observation Inventory is related to the observer. In the Inventory, the descriptive data are obtained by one or more observers, while in the Interview the interviewed individual reports his observations (Wolman, 1978).

The observations can be tabulated in accordance with the

estimates of power and of acceptance of self and others. What does the subject think of himself? Does he believe himself to be active, alert, efficient? Or, outside these clues, does he believe himself to be intelligent, good-looking, successful, etc.?

These self-ratings are not objective measurements of personality. They are merely patterns of self-rating that will go up in hyperinstrumentals whenever they experience tangible success, will fluctuate rapidly in dysmutuals, and will be persistently low in hypervectorials.

In describing others, hyperinstrumentals will give scanty, rather mechanized descriptions, such as "the girl in the office," "the supervisor," etc., while hypervectorials will spend a great deal of time talking about others and describing their feelings. Dysmutuals will most often resemble the hyperinstrumentals in their egocentric talk but will pay more attention to the feelings of others.

Hypervectorials tend to criticize themselves and avoid criticizing others; when they hate, they tend to develop projective mechanisms and claim that others hate them. When they talk about parents and other relatives, they use a great deal of caution. Hyperinstrumentals speak frankly and critically about whomever they dislike; they find their hostility justified and give a frank, though often distorted, picture of interaction with others. Dysmutuals are more critical than the other two types. They blame everyone, including themselves, are highly opinionated, and label others. They either praise or condemn, and their story is full of value judgment. When they repeat the same detail in a subsequent interview, the two accounts rarely resemble each other.

14

Neuropharmacological Treatment

MIND-BODY DICHOTOMY

In dealing with the treatment of mental disorders one cannot ignore the mind-body dichotomy. It is an obvious fact that nature frequently crosses the bridge linking the mind to the body. This bridge is crossed from mind to body in a variety of psychosomatic disorders and from body to mind in innumerable physical ailments and in the use and abuse of drugs. Sociopaths are particularly inclined to develop psychosomatic symptoms. They are, however, not the only ones prone to psychosomatics, for practically every mental disorder can lead to a variety of physical symptoms used as a cover, escape, or defense against anxiety, depression, anger, and so on. On the other hand, almost every physical ailment can make one frustrated, worried, apprehensive, anxious, depressed, and prone to irrational mental processes. Almost all drugs affect one's feeling about oneself and can stimulate or suppress agitation, sensitivity, withdrawal, or aggressiveness.

Small wonder that a variety of physicochemical methods are used in the treatment of mental disorders including antisocial personality (Leventhal, 1984). Neuro- and psychopharmacological methods are quite successful in controlling a variety of symptoms and are, therefore, widely used by the therapeutic professions in the treatment of almost all mental disorders. Human behavior is somatopsychic and psychosomatic, and one may use psychological methods in physical diseases in order to strengthen one's immune system and resilience and use physicochemical methods in the treatment of mental disorders. Certainly, one cannot cure an infectious disease by using psychological methods, but one can definitely control mental disorder with physicochemical treatment methods.

PHARMACOLOGICAL TREATMENT

It is an open question whether neuropharmacology can cure schizophrenia or manic-depressive psychosis. The concept of cure is not clear in mental disorders as it is clear in physical ailments. Obviously one does or does not *have* measles or pneumonia, but one *is* a schizophrenic or a sociopath. The difference has far-reaching consequences. It might be convenient to assume that in mental disorders a lifelong disappearance of symptoms and adequate adjustment are tantamount to cure, but one can never be sure whether the predisposition to reappearance of the symptoms was ever completely eradicated. However, suppression of antisocial behavior is an important step in the right direction, and the more lasting are the effects of pharmacological methods, the more reasons for their use.

There is some evidence that acting-out, impulsive, and aggressive sociopaths can benefit by treatment with lithium carbonate and tricyclic antidepressants (Eichelman et al., 1981; Sandler, 1979). Serotonin is an inhibitory neurotransmitter and may at least partially inhibit catecholamine-induced impulsive and aggressive behaviors. Electrical stimulation of brain serotonergic areas tends to suppress aggressiveness (Kostowski et al., 1980), but it is not sure how much and for how long.

Anticonvulsants are often used with aggressive patients, especially those who had or were suspected of having seizures. Neuroleptic drugs, the phenothiazines, such as chlorpromazine decrease aggressive behavior. Also, butyrophenones inhibit agitation and violence, but they may induce cerebral dysrhythmias and tardive dyskinesia (Gualtieri et al., 1980; Moyers, 1976). Most neuroleptics have been quite successful in controlling aggressive behavior in children and adolescents. Psychostimulants such as amphetamines contribute to aggressive and violent behavior, whereas haloperidol and other dopamine blockers are among widely used neuroleptics that control impulsive and aggressive behavior. Several studies pointed to the effectiveness of propranolol in treatment of antisocial and aggressive behavior (Schreier, 1979; Williams et al., 1982; Yudofsky et al., 1981).

Minor tranquilizers, especially diazepam and chlordiazepoxide, are frequently used in controlling aggressive behavior. However, their efficacy and lasting effect are not proven. Some studies indicate that diazepam and chlordiazepoxide stimulate hostile behavior. Adrenergic blockers, especially propranolol, are believed to inhibit aggressive impulses (Weinstock & Weiss, 1980) and, as mentioned above, have been widely used (Williams et al., 1982).

Many antidepressants act on serotonergic and noradrenergic systems and should be counterindicated in the treatment of violence. There is some evidence they could facilitate aggression (Maj et al., 1980; Rampling, 1978).

It must be stressed that the various pharmacological devices are symptom-specific and not diagnosis-specific. They can control symptoms but they cannot cure personality disorders. Some of the above-mentioned drugs can control antisocial aggressive behavior, but it is questionable whether they could cure the antisocial sociopathic personality.

A good summary of the usefulness of the various neuropharmacological methods was given by Leventhal (1984, pp. 333–334). It is quoted below with some abbreviations:

> 1) *Lithium carbonate* is a drug of major promise for adolescents and adults. Its usefulness can be deduced from the neuropharmacological action of lithium as it affects behavior.

Clinical trials, in addition, have confirmed the potential efficacy of this compound.

2) *Propranolol*, likewise, appears to have real potential in the management of aggression. Studies still in progress direct our attention to the usefulness of this drug with adolescents.

3) *Antipsychotic medications* including phenothiazines, butyrophenones, thioxanthines, and oxyindoles appear to have possible benefits for treatment of both violent nonpsychotic and psychotic patients. The risk of tardive dyskinesia attendant to long-term use of those drugs should give the clinician a warning. Short-term treatment or the absence of other available medications seem the only justifiable grounds for the employment of these drugs.

4) The *anticonvulsants*, diphenylhydantoin or phenytoin and carbamazepine, have demonstrated ability to control some forms of violent and aggressive behavior and are especially useful when the behaviors are episodic or associated with EEG abnormalities. (Note that the latter are not necessary conditions for these agents to be effective.) Carbamazepine, in particular, which appears to be relatively nontoxic, may be a very useful agent in the treatment of violent and aggressive behavior.

5) *Antidepressants* may be effective in the control of violence when it is seen in conjunction with diagnosable depressive disorders. In the absence of such a diagnosis, however, the risk of actually facilitating the aggressive and violent behavior may discourage the clinician from administering these medications.

6) The *psychostimulant* medications appear to have a very circumscribed role in the treatment of violence; their usefulness is limited to the ADD (MBD) patient. The inherent (albeit small) risk of precipitating a paranoid psychosis with these agents is outweighed in cases where the individuals show chronically aggressive behavior accompanying antisocial or asocial activities and a past history of ADD.

7) *Minor tranquilizers* (the benzodiazepines specifically) probably have only a very limited role in the management of violent and aggressive behavior; there is, in fact, strong indication that they may even potentiate aggressive behavior. The exceptions are the cases of individuals who demonstrate a clear anxiety syndrome or—possibly—as an adjunct to the treatment of LSD or PCP intoxication.

8) *Antiandrogen and progesteronal* agents do not appear to have any role in the management of violence or aggression in adolescents. They appear to be effective only for the treatment of certain kinds of male sex offenders. Hormonal manipulation of behavior disorders related to premenstrual tension is not available for adolescents.

15

Psychoanalysis and Related Methods

In 1935, August Aichhorn, director of an institution for delinquent youth, published the book *Wayward Youth*, in which he described the application of the psychoanalytic method to antisocial adolescents. As mentioned previously, Aichhorn drew a distinction between three types of antisocial behavior and suggested three different methods of treatment. Individuals who were "criminals from a sense of guilt" belonged to the first type. According to Sigmund Freud, some individuals, driven by a severe guilt feeling originated in their harsh superego, turn to delinquent behavior in order to be punished and thus alleviate their guilt feelings. Aichhorn recommended psychoanalytic treatment for this type of antisocial behavior.

The antisocial adolescents who have identified themselves with their antisocial parents and have developed a "nonsocial superego" needed a modified psychoanalytic technique. The main task was to encourage a strong positive transference to the therapist, who should use a variety of incentives including unconditional forgiveness and admiration and even gifts. These parameters led to identification with the therapist and fostered the development of a normal superego.

The "primitive delinquents" who had no superego belonged to Aichhorn's third type. Aichhorn suggested institutional treatment for them. He believed that they needed a structured environment in which they should receive a nonpunitive and nonpsychoanalytic psychotherapy.

Apparently, Aichhorn's delinquents of the first type were not sociopaths. Probably they were borderline, schizoid individuals or full-blown schizophrenics (I call them "hypervectorials"), who, driven by a strong guilt feeling, acted out to provoke punishment (Wolman, 1970, 1973). Aichhorn's second and third types of delinquents were definitely sociopaths either with a faulty superego (the second type) or with no superego (the third type).

Almost at the same time, Alexander and Healy (1935) embarked on a psychoanalytic research and treatment project of antisocial individuals in the United States. The psychoanalytic treatment in prisons brought limited success; Alexander and Healy blamed the restrictive and punitive prison environment for the lack of success. They believed that the patients should be allowed to leave the prisons, become gainfully employed, and start a normal life in a normal environment. A normal environment would enable the patients to benefit by psychoanalysis.

In further research and treatment of 143 delinquents, Healy and Bronner (1936) diagnosed 26 patients as psychotics and only five of them have shown any improvement. The antisocial patients who came from highly disturbed families and/or delinquent neighborhoods have made little progress in psychoanalytic psychotherapy. A wholesome parent-child relationship was conducive to therapeutic progress. Alexander and Healy introduced a flexible approach to the psychoanalytic technique, following Alexander's method of manipulating transference.

According to Dalmau (1961), the psychopath's symbolic behavior is regressive. It involves genital-sadistic attacks against society and shifts to an anal homosexual need to be "screwed" and taken care of. Psychoanalytic treatment should introject the superego. The emergence of psychosomatic symptoms and anxiety is indicative of therapeutic progress, for they are indicative of an emerging superego.

Chwast (1972) reported his therapeutic work with sociopaths at the clinic of the Association for the Psychiatric Treatment of Offenders. He applied a psychoanalytically oriented method of treatment. He stressed the maintenance of friendly rapport with the patients, realistic setting of goals, concrete assistance, uncovering of the patients' maneuvers, continuous encouragement, and support of developing positive social attachments.

Schmideberg (1961) noticed that although sociopaths often act in impulsive and self-destructive manners, suicide among them is exceedingly rare. Sociopaths are sadistic, they do not want to change, they expect disproportionate praise and reward for whatever they do. They tend to manipulate psychotherapy and misinterpret whatever insight is offered to them. Schmideberg believes that success in psychotherapy is possible only in a restricted situation, when the psychopath is obliged to undergo psychotherapy under a threat of punishment.

Eissler's (1949) *Searchlights on Delinquency* utilized some of Aichhorn's ideas and followed Heinz Hartmann's principles of ego psychology. While adhering to the fundamental principles of classic psychoanalysis, Eissler suggested necessary modifications (parameters) in the treatment of antisocial adolescents.

Masterson (1980) maintained that some antisocial individuals should be treated as outpatients, but the severely disturbed, acting-out aggressive adolescents and adults need a firm environmental structure and must be institutionalized. Their hospital treatment must be combined with intensive family therapy.

Many psychoanalysts were disappointed with the results of psychoanalysis and psychoanalytically oriented psychotherapy with sociopaths. According to P. F. Kernberg (1977), psychoanalysis is counterindicated for "severe narcissistic personalities, antisocial character structure and drug addiction" (p. 400). This opinion is also held by other experts who conclude: "The treatment of antisocial personality includes psychotherapy, behavior therapy, pharmacological therapy, electroconvulsive therapy, lobotomy and imprisonment. None of these has been shown to be effective and the illness still does not have a successful treatment" (Robins, 1977, p. 365).

16

Behavior Modification and Related Methods

The term "behavioral therapy" was introduced in 1958 by A. A. Lazarus when he described J. Wolpe's "objective psychotherapy." At present, the various behavioral techniques are widely used in treatment of practically all types of mental disorders (Wilson & Lazarus, 1983).

Behavioral treatment uses several techniques, among them (1) positive reinforcement, (2) negative reinforcement, (3) aversion conditioning, (4) withdrawal of positive stimulation, and (5) extinction, that is, discontinuation of reinforcement. The first two methods belong to the acceleration technique; the last three methods are deceleration techniques.

Behavioral treatment methods usually have a better chance in a residential or institutional environment than in any type of outpatient setting (Moss & Rick, 1981). Whatever behavioral method is applied, it requires some degree of compliance and subordination on the part of its recipients. Institutional settings provide a better opportunity for cooperation, compliance, and subordination, and the term "resistance" applies also to behavioral treatment:

> The concept of "resistance" (behavioral nonresponsiveness) has become as important to behavior therapists as it has been for psychoanalysts, although their respective views on

the subject differ markedly. Significant aspects of control and countercontrol should not be overlooked, as Lazarus and Fay (1982) emphasize, and from a behavioral perspective, the varieties of resistance may be attributed to four main factors:
1) Resistance as a function of the patient's individual characteristics.
2) Resistance as a product of the patient's interpersonal relationships (systems or family processes).
3) Resistance as a function of the therapist (or the relationship).
4) Resistance as a function of the state of the art (and science).

Lazarus and Fay (1982) elaborate on each of these areas and offer the caveat that a vague and general usage of "resistance" is more likely to obfuscate than illuminate the course of therapeutic endeavors. Some therapists tend to confuse resistance with rationalized failure.

It is easy to offer various post hoc explanations according to learning principles, but it is obviously useless to do so in terms of their predictive value. When examining therapeutic failures, to insist that target behaviors did not shift in a desired direction because the maintaining conditions and requisite reinforcements were inadequately manipulated, may be true in some instances. (Wilson & Lazarus, 1983, p. 126)

POSITIVE REINFORCEMENT

The technique of positive reinforcement applies the principles of operant conditioning and is used as a method of material as well as symbolic rewards given by the therapist to patients in order to encourage socially acceptable behavior. Dealing with antisocial children, adolescents, and, occasionally, adults, therapists use material reinforcers, such as gifts and money. The symbolic reinforcers include praise, tokens for good behavior, and so on. A combination of material and symbolic reinforcers was successfully used in behavior therapy with adolescents (Moss & Rick, 1981).

The positive reinforcement method can be used in two ways: 1) Social and symbolic reinforcers are usually more effective and give more lasting results. Since all sociopaths suffer from some degree of inferiority feelings, the positive social reinforcers method uses praise, paying attention, approval, recognition and respect for whatever good qualities and achievements the patient has. Boosting their self-respect reduces their need for antisocial and exaggerated self-assertive behavior. 2) In many instances, especially with adolescents, material reinforcers such as small gifts and money, as well as activity reinforcers such as free time, trips, games and so on, are used in behavior therapy. (Bandura, 1969)

Many antisocial adolescents act cautiously in regard to people they fear, such as court-appointed counselors, district attorneys, and school principals. They are polite and respectful and try to make a good impression on powerful authoritative figures, but act in a totally disrespectful manner with no consideration for people they do not fear, like peers, parents, and teachers. Positive reinforcement is used to modify their behavior in regard to everybody, and often it does work.

TOKEN ECONOMY

Token-economies programs and the point-levels systems are also an application of operant conditioning. Wilson and Lazarus (1983, pp. 140–141) describe them as follows:

> Although the procedures and goals of the many procedures subsumed under the rubric of token economy programs may vary, they all share the following common defining characteristics. First, the specific behaviors that are to be modified or developed have to be identified and operationally defined. Typical target behaviors would include self-care behaviors in psychotic patients or improved academic performance in children. Second, the available reinforcers in the environment have to be determined. Reinforcers are the "good things in life" that people are willing to work for. In the case of the hospital patient these might range from such fundamental privileges as watching T.V. or securing a private room. For the child in the classroom a reinforcer might be candy, toys or extra recess time. Third, there are the tokens themselves. The token is a compound discriminative and secondary rein-

forcer that stands for the back-up reinforcers. The advantages of using tokens as reinforcers are that they bridge the gap between the target behavior and the back-up reinforcers, they permit the reinforcement of any response at any time, and they provide the same reward for patients who have different preferences in back-up reinforcers. The token itself might be a tangible item such as a poker chip or a plastic card, or else it might be a checkmark on a piece of paper. Finally, there are the exchange rules of the program, that is, how tokens may be earned and the cost of the back-up reinforcers. These exchange rules involve complex relationships that have been analyzed in terms of, and compared to, the economic principles governing real-life society outside of the immediate token economy environment. Although token economy procedures have often been described in oversimplified reinforcement terms, they incorporate many social influence processes including operant and classical conditioning, social reinforcement, modeling and expectancy of success. Within this general social influence context the specific token reinforcement contingencies play the decisive role in regulating behavior change.

Contrary to the frequently expressed criticism that token programs are simplistic, impersonal and mechanistic, their successful implementation demands a wide range of clinical skills, including flexibility, creativity, perseverance, and "canny know-how" on the part of the behavior therapist. Perhaps the most formidable task involves staff training. The operation of the token program, and indeed all operant-based behavior modification procedures, can best be understood in terms of Tharp and Wetzel's (1969) triadic model of treatment intervention. According to this model, the therapist functions as a *consultant* who possesses the necessary knowledge of how to formulate and plan behavior change programs. These plans are then implemented by the mediators, those people who have the closest contact with the *target*—anyone who has a problem to be modified. Mediators may be parents, teachers, peers, nurses, attendants or employers—in fact, anyone who is in a position to control the important reinforcement contingencies in the target's environment.

NEGATIVE REINFORCEMENT

The aim of negative reinforcement is to encourage avoidance and escape behavior; it means using punishment that forces avoidance behavior. The therapist explains to the patients the negative consequences of their behavior in regard to themselves and to people they care for.

Using punishment, and especially corporal punishment, is an ethically controversial method, and it certainly does not work with adolescent or adult sociopaths. Punishment increases their feeling of being innocently and unfairly treated; thus it encourages their wish to fight back and hurt others. Criticism, rejection, and punishment makes them more angry, more vindictive, and more violent (Agee, 1979).

WITHDRAWAL AND POSITIVE REINFORCEMENT

Taking away privileges in an institutional setting may produce some results. It can be divided into "time-out" and "response cost" techniques. Both methods have been used in institutional settings with acting-out adolescents. Time out from positive reinforcement implies a brief period (5–15 min) of isolation from the peer group as a mild punishment for inappropriate behavior. Response cost implies loss of points, or tokens or any other reward, until there is a significant change in behavior. Many years ago when I was director of an institution for disturbed children and adolescents, I used the time-out method with a 14-year-old psychopathic boy who terrorized his peers. There has been some success; however, it could not be determined whether the effect of the treatment was permanent.

SELF-CONTROL METHODS

In the self-control technique the individuals are taught to manipulate their own behavior. They are guided to use self-punishment after inappropriate behavior and self-reinforcement after appropriate behavior. Self-control methods often are used as a continuation of the token-economy method, when the individual does not need to receive points any longer and praise for his or her behavior; it can also be used instead of self-regulation and self-praise. This method has been used with adults, adolescents, and even children (Bandura, 1969; Lochman et al., 1980).

COGNITIVE BEHAVIOR THERAPY

Cognitive behavior therapy has been used in treatment of mental disorders, including antisocial personality. Wilson and O'Leary (1980, p. 280) compared the efficiency of cognitive behavior therapy and psychoanalytic methods as follows:

> a) Cognitive methods in behavior therapy are concerned primarily with conscious thought processes, rather than unconscious, symbolic meanings; b) cognitive methods in behavior therapy emphasize the regulatory influence of current cognitions. It is unnecessary to determine the unconscious roots of inaccurate or irrational interpretations of reality. It is a general characteristic of behavior therapy that the therapist focuses on how the client distorts cognitively and what to do about it, rather than on why the distortion occurs; c) cognitive methods in behavior therapy are explicitly formulated and testable in contrast to the looser, more vaguely formulated concepts in psychodynamic approaches; d) initial studies show that some cognitive methods in behavior therapy appear to be more efficient and effective than psychoanalytically-oriented treatment.

RESULT OF TREATMENT

Behavior therapy has been quite successful in extinction of sexual deviations (Callahan & Leitenberg, 1973; Fookes, 1969). However, so far behavior therapy is not always successful with aggressive, violent sociopaths (Goldstone, 1983). According to Goldstone, we do not have adequate treatment methods for antisocial behavior. Thus, he writes, "Unless we limit our discussion of antisocial behavior to the few exotic cases that apparently responded to aversive problems, confinement treats the effects, not the behavior" (pp. 463–464). According to Goldstone:

> Antisocial behavior has been viewed as a learning disability subject to specific training procedures: as an insufficiency of arousal and stimulus deprivation requiring a continued infusion of motivation and affective supplies. It has been viewed from the standpoint of deviant memory, attention, or information processing; as a product of toxic families due to loss, separation, rejection, brutality, uncertainty, or defective genes; and as a structural or functional disorder of the brain. These distinctions are heuristically useful, and have been valuable in the scientific study of psychopathic personalities and antisocial behavior. Each provides a solid bedrock of tradition and technique for studying different aspects of life touching all strata from the molecular to the social.

Apparently, the treatment of sociopathic, antisocial individuals is not as successful as the treatment of other mental disorders, no matter what the theoretical premises of the therapists are or the particular method they use.

17

Interactional Psychotherapy

Sociopaths reluctantly go for psychotherapeutic treatment. They do not believe that there is anything wrong with them, and they feel that they are always innocent. A patient who was brought to the hospital by the police after he split his wife's head with a hammer was sure that he had the right to do so. He turned to the resident psychiatrist with an innocent question: "Doc, wouldn't you have done the same?"

Sociopaths may, however, come voluntarily, provided: (1) someone else pays for the treatment, (2) they are afflicted by a true or imaginary physical disease and their doctor told them that it was psychosomatic, and (3) they expect to gain something by playing the "sick role."

Maturity is synonymous with responsibility. Responsibility means the willingness to do the things one wants and to accept the possible consequences. Most sociopaths do what they can as long as they believe they can "get away with murder." They usually believe they can do this, and they are often unaware that whatever one does will have certain consequences. They somehow assume that they can outsmart everyone and thus compensate for their basic feelings of inferiority. Psychotherapy with the hyperinstrumental (sociopathic) type is not an easy task.

I once had in treatment a young businessman who was

cheating his customers and partners, and who justified his actions by saying, "If they are so dumb as to allow me to cheat, they deserve it. It is tough luck!" I asked him whether he checked my monthly bills. "No," he said with a smile, "I trust you." "Well," I said, "I will tell my secretary to inflate the bills. If you don't check them, you deserve to be cheated. Tough!" "Doctor Wolman," he exclaimed, "I would lose all respect I have for you!" "Okay, and what do you think of my respect for you?" I asked.

Psychotherapy with sociopaths presents a challenge to the therapist's skills, patience, and self-confidence. All sociopaths are notoriously dishonest and do not honor the agreements concerning their fees. Almost all of them are selfish and parasitic and rarely, if ever, keep their promises. In my private practice the sociopathic patients are the only ones who do not pay their bills and claim nonexisting hardships for breaking their promises.

TRANSFERENCE

Sociopaths tend to develop negative transference and transfer to the therapist the hatred they harbored against their parents. "My father didn't care for me," said a 40-year-old man, "and you are a copy of my father. You feel nothing for me. I am just one of the score of your patients. You have no compassion for me," he complained.

Suffering is the main motive for seeking professional help. Small wonder that hyperinstrumentals (sociopaths) rarely seek help. They have little reason to, for they rarely suffer severe inner conflicts; as a rule, they make others suffer. Being highly self-cathected, these individuals may occasionally suffer from hypochondriacal fears, anxiety states caused by erupting id impulses, and inferiority feelings stemming from defeat or frustration. They may also seek secondary gain by assuming the sick role or wearing the mask of innocent victims of misfortune. When they come for help, they seek immediate results and are likely to break off the therapy as soon as they feel better.

In some Veterans Administration hospitals hyperinstrumentals have become hard-core cases who resist any therapy. They often prefer staying in the hospital and continuing a parasitic life. One of my sociopathic patients used to hospitalize himself frequently with a variety of imaginary illnesses. Whenever he faced difficulties in business or in marital life, he escaped into illness. He came to me for treatment to "get something out of it" and to "get the right guidance." He bragged to everyone that he had serious mental problems and was undergoing psychoanalysis.

Sociopaths on all five levels are not inclined to invest their libido in anyone, and their transference, if any, stays shallow. Whereas I recommend prevention of too deep a transference in hypervectorials, the crucial task with hyperinstrumentals is to foster as deep a transference as possible and mollify their negative transference. Needless to say, the sociopaths-hyperinstrumentals hate whoever frustrates their wishes for immediate gratification.

Manipulation of transference in these cases is not an easy task. Hyperinstrumentals learned in childhood to defend themselves against rejecting, absentee, or overindulgent parents. In any case, the prehyperinstrumental has never had the opportunity to identify with either of his parents. Although hyperinstrumentals are usually aggressive, they perceive themselves as defenseless, innocent children. This attitude colors their oral-aggressive negative transference in psychotherapy.

One patient spent hour after hour directing the most malicious accusations at me. Whatever wrong had been done to her by her parents (truly or in her imagination) was ascribed to me. She expected retaliation on my part, which, of course, never came. Her amazement at the lack of hostility was, as Alexander would put it, "a therapeutic corrective experience" (Alexander & French, 1946).

Another patient described his fantastically ingenious deceits and frauds. "Everybody does it, don't they?" he asked. His father and mother had been exceedingly permissive, but the outer world was less permissive; he was caught and punished. He believed that the world was hostile to him and he developed paranoid fears.

Whoever treats sociopaths cannot stay neutral. Normality includes social adjustment and a reasonable balance of inter- and intraindividual cathexes: it includes a balanced love for oneself and others, as well as a balanced criticism of oneself and others. A rational superego is an indispensable part of a healthy personality. Thus, the therapist faces a complex task: silent permissiveness may be misinterpreted as siding with the id, but an expression of disapproval by the therapist is not good either, for this may lead to the inclusion of the therapist in the paranoid picture of world conspiracy against the poor, innocent patient. The therapist must take a stand and help in developing the patient's superego, but he must wait until a positive transference is sufficiently strong. Interpretation must wait until the patient is ready to accept it, and even then, firmness must be combined with caution. An exceedingly active or passive intervention, as well as one which is too early and too active, may lead to a breaking off of treatment.

Sociopaths tend to project their own selfishness and dishonesty on everyone and frequently on the therapist. The therapist must avoid being trapped by the sociopath's manipulations. Some of them promise to cooperate with the therapist in order to win concessions; when they fail, they lash out with accusations: "You could not see me when I called you in despair," a 28-year-old woman screamed. "You really don't care for anyone. You are self-satisfied and selfish!"

The therapist must not get involved in defensive explanations. He or she must retain a cool, objective, and helping attitude. Whereas one must avoid too much interpretation with patients (schizoids and schizophrenics), one need not spare interpretation with hyperinstrumentals-sociopaths.

SOCIOPATHS' MANIPULATIONS

The so-called "charming sociopaths" try to charm and outsmart the doctor. The sociopaths pretend to cooperate and describe in detail their sexual experiences, financial manipulations, and interpersonal encounters. They pretend to be always the innocent victims forced to defend themselves. They never did anything wrong, and if they occasionally erred, the good God and the good doctor should understand and forgive. They often try to win over the therapist and make him their ally against their parents, spouses, and other "enemies." Quite often sociopathic patients turn to the therapist with a shrewd question: "Wouldn't you do the same if your spouse [or relative or partner] did to you what they did to me?"

Some sociopaths are bright, some average, some below average. The IQ is not related to personality traits and mental health (Wolman, 1985), but bright sociopaths are sometimes successful in outsmarting their psychiatrists and psychologists. They play on their doctors' curiosity, exploit their willingness to help, and play on their natural compassionate attitude. Many sociopaths show a phony concern for the doctor's well-being, shower him or her with praises and flattery, and even bring little gifts. They try, often successfully, to make a good impression that will enable them to manipulate the psychotherapist.

THE THERAPIST'S FIRM ATTITUDE

Carney (1977) described the treatment problems of a speical offenders clinic, which treats violent offenders who are on probation. An authoritarian attitude and imposing of limits, as a rule, bring better results than a permissive attitude.

It seems that in most instances, authoritarian therapy, with the therapist playing the role of a concerned but no-nonsense parent, brings better results than the traditional, permissive psychotherapy. Sociopaths have little, if any, respect for moral values, and they perceive kindness as a sign of weakness and suspect vested interest in charitable deeds. They do not believe that anyone would do anything for anyone without apparent or hidden gains.

Power is the only thing sociopaths believe in, respect, and fear. A friendly, but at the same time stern and forceful therapist can make a dent in their attitude. In some cases they may accept the therapist as their role-model and develop an admiring attitude toward him. This new attitude of *identification* with the therapist hardly resembles the usual transference, but it is the key to successful psychotherapy.

Quite often, when sociopaths' freedom of action is curtailed, they tend to develop psychosomatic symptoms and depressive moods. They unconsciously regress to infantile behavior; when the tantrums are curtailed, many an infant feels very upset, very weak, and ill. Restrainment often brings a similar reaction in adult sociopaths.

Sometimes when they improve in therapy and begin to control their acting-out, they may react with depression and psychosomatic symptoms. Anger and verbal and/or physical acting-out give the sociopaths the feeling of power they crave. The self-imposed restraint often leads to the feeling of being weak and creates depression; depression is a feeling of helplessness associated with self-directed anger and blaming oneself for being weak, and psychosomatic symptoms call for the therapist's compassion. Here is a quote from a a 40-year-old sociopath:

> I feel like a weakling, a nothing. They can do as they please, and I am supposed to take it and not fight! What do you want from me?! I am a man, a real man, and I feel like killing all of them. Why are you telling me to be rational! Dr. Wolman, I know that you are right and ask me to be rational, but I am getting furious, very depressed, and develop all kinds of pain!

The only way the therapist should react to this outburst is to remain calm and firm. The therapist must demand self-control, and he offers praise for whatever degree of self-control the patient shows and suggests a positive and rational way of behavior. Reality testing is the clue to rational behavior.

REALITY TESTING

One of the chief principles in working with sociopaths is a continuous and relentless *reality testing*. The patient must be continuously confronted, not with the mistrust but with the necessity to check his or her story. The checking must be detailed and exacting and conducted in a nonemotional, matter-of-fact manner. I usually repeat to the patients that whatever conclusions they reach and whatever action they take, they must be absolutely sure about what has happened and the details on which they intend to act. In other words, I avoid dealing with the moral superego aspects of the problem alien to the sociopaths and stick to realistic, ego aspects of their life. Only toward the end of successful psychotherapy, when an adequate identification with the therapist has taken place, may one expect the beginning of moral behavior.

MUTUAL TRUST

Ultimately, the success of therapeutic interaction depends on *mutual trust* between the therapist and the patient. The lack of trust in anyone is the main stumbling block in working with sociopaths. Sociopaths don't trust anyone; they suspect everybody. As mentioned above, paranoia is one of the outstanding symptoms of sociopathic personality.

On the other hand, it is not easy for therapists to trust their sociopathic patients. Sociopaths try to manipulate the therapists. They lie whenever it fits their mood or purpose. They pretend obedience and cooperation and act in a manner aimed at impressing the therapist. A two-way interaction is necessary. On one hand, the therapist continuously scrutinizes the patient's communication. This must be done in an inoffensive, matter-of-fact, reality-testing manner that shows the patient that the therapist is not a "naive, stupid, shrink," but a firm and wise friend. On the other hand, the patient has the right to check whatever the therapist says. The therapist never lies and is never evasive, and when he commits an error, he admits it. Such a two-way interaction facilitates the process of identification with the therapist and formation of a superego.

THERAPEUTIC SUCCESS

There are cases of successful psychotherapy with nonviolent sociopaths, although they are the minority and are greatly dependent on the sociopaths' awareness of the beneficial impact of therapeutic work. Mr. S. was a bright, 22-year-old drifter with a college degree, who held a menial job in New York City administration. He came late to work, asking someone else to punch his card. He took long coffee breaks and conducted long personal telephone calls. When he was asked to go on an official visit, he spent hours in a movie and filed a phone report. In short, the amount of his productive work was quite low, but he knew how to "butter up his superiors and bullshit his way through."

He was bored with his job. He felt he was going nowhere and was annoyed with his meager salary. He came for therapy complaining about a nonexisting physical disease, but as long as the City paid for most of his therapy and his father paid the balance, he did not mind being out of his dull office and talking to a friendly doctor twice a week.

I decided to utilize his boredom. I sought to find out whether he had any interests that could be of help in therapy. Fortunately, he loved photography and television. I guided him in this direction, and he registered in an evening program in a college. He enjoyed it and made good progress. He was grateful to me and to his professors. He began to realize that not everybody was out to loot him, and there are people willing to help others. It was a slow process of learning and readjustment, and his self-attitude has gradually changed from exploiting to give-and-take relationships. Was he cured? I doubt it, but he was definitely much improved.

Unfortunately, sociopaths do not last too long in therapy,

especially if they have to pay for it. Usually they develop a negative transference and project their selfish, exploitative attitude on the psychotherapist. They expect unconditional approval of their self-righteous behavior and often quit therapy before significant progress is made.

18

Family and Group Therapies

THE ROLE OF THE FAMILY

There are several different approaches to family therapy, such as behavioral, psychodynamic, cognitive, contextual, structural, family, therapy as a theory of roles and values, multiple family group therapy (MFGT), and others (Wolman & Stricker, 1983). At the present time, all psychotherapeutic methods have a close affinity to one or more of the family therapy methods, for it is rather difficult to treat mental disorders outside the family context.

In Freud's time members of the same family were treated by different therapists. This sometimes may lead to misinformation of the therapists; for instance, patient A told one story to "his doctor," and the spouse or the offspring told another story to "their doctor." Quite often the patients confronted each other misquoting the utterances of the doctors, thus unwillingly and unwittingly disturbing the treatment process.

Most, if not all, emotional difficulties start in childhood, and no therapeutic method can afford to ignore the patients' past experiences. Treatment of the members of the same family by *one* therapist substantially reduces the danger of miscommunication, misinformation, and confusion. Thus, every psychotherapy is indeed a sort of family therapy, whether the members of the same family are treated separately, conjointly, or together with outsiders in the MFGT therapy. The decision of which method to use is up to the psychiatrist, psychologist, or psychiatric social worker who conducts the therapy, but the decision must not be solely dependent on the therapist's theoretical orientation. The type and the level of antisocial behavior, the ages of the family members, and their interrelationship must be considered. The socioeconomic status, the neighborhood, and other environmental factors should be considered. However, the *personality* of the therapist is undoubtedly the single most important factor that outweighs his or her theoretical beliefs and preferred technique, be it behavioral, psychoanalytic, or any other. Psychotherapy is always a process of human interaction, and every human being and, obviously every therapist is a different person (Wolman, 1984a).

Sometimes it may be advisable to practice family therapy with a sociopath on a one-to-one basis. I tried once to bring together the father, the mother, the teen-age son, and the daughter. The family therapy session was controlled by the father's dictatorial and threatening sermon, and no one else dared to contradict him out of fear of physical violence. The son was originally assigned for therapy because of several petty thefts, truancy, and cheating in school, but the father's selfish, self-righteous, and violent behavior disrupted the therapeutic sessions. I had another case of treatment of a family as a unit which failed because of screaming matches between the parents. However, even in working on a one-to-one basis, an occasional family confrontation session could be advisable.

In some instances continuous sessions with the entire family are indicated and could be productive. When the level of antisocial behavior is low and there is little verbal abuse and no violence, the participation of the entire family can be useful. Sometimes the family can be treated in family-therapy sessions in *addition* to individual sessions with the individual family members. Sociopaths tend to act out and are often hostile to other members of their family, and they usually need individual attention in addition to or prior to the joint session with the other family members.

One may expect less difficulty in working with the so-called "charming sociopaths" for they are usually polite to the other family members. In family sessions they may try to outshine and outsmart the others and hope the therapist will accept their lies and side with them against the other family members.

FAMILY THERAPY WITH ACTING-OUT SOCIOPATHS

It is much more difficult to work with acting-out and violent sociopaths of any age, children, adolescents, or adults. The decline in family cohesiveness, the alienation in intramarital relationships, the growing rate of divorce, and the increased frequency of violent behavior militate for family therapy, but make it more difficult (Wolman & Stricker, 1983). I have tried, unsuccessfully, family therapy with an acting-out family and had to give it up after a few stormy sessions.

Usually, the beginnings are most difficult. Unless forced by a court order, most families with one or more acting-out sociopaths refuse to undergo family therapy. If they do agree, they view the family psychotherapy as a forum for expressing their grievances and venting their hostilities. They come to the family therapy sessions ready to accuse each other of verbal and physical abuse, and they continue the abusive behavior in the presence of the therapist.

Robin (1981) analyzed the results of family therapeutic efforts aimed at improving communication between the parents and the acting-out antisocial adolescents. His cognitive-behavior therapy method stresses the need for such an improvement, for rational communication is believed to be a prerequisite for conflict resolution. Moss and Rick (1981) described the operant condition "token-economies" method;

this method was applied by the Oregon Research Institute in their work with the parents of antisocial violent children (Patterson, 1975). There is, however, no proof that these and other methods used in family therapy have brought satisfactory results.

As mentioned above, most of these families refuse to undergo family therapy and/or discontinue it after a few sessions. Weathers and Liberman (1975) reported family therapy with 28 families of adolescent delinquents and their parents: only 6 of 28 families completed three sessions, and 16 completed one session only.

Somewhat better results were reported by Gant et al. (1981), who worked with 10 court-referred families. All 10 families were low-middle-class. The family-therapy sessions were conducted in the homes of the families by a team of therapists for seven months. Apparently, the court order was of great help, and probably the participation of more than one therapist was quite useful.

Treatment of violence in intrafamilial relations was described by Barnhill (1980). There were five stages in the therapeutic process, namely, (1) separating of the adversaries, (2) "no-violence contact" with unlimited access to the therapist, (3) full access to family physician, social worker, and school authorities, (4) short-term treatment, and (5) referral for more profound, long-term therapy. This approach was utilized in the framework of a community mental health center; it is rather doubtful whether this approach could work outside community-based and/or court-related programs.

GROUP THERAPY

There are several types of group therapy, among them (in alphabetical order) activity, behavioral, encounter, gestalt, intensive, interactional, marathon, psychoanalytical, psychodrama, repressive-inspirational, social-club, and transactional (Rosenbaum, 1983). Some of the above-mentioned methods have been used in the treatment of antisocial adolescents and adults with mixed outcomes. According to Rosenbaum (p. 222):

> Clinical practitioners may be overwhelmed by the proliferation of group techniques that are classified as group therapy. The field of group psychotherapy continues to grow, and this growth has been in the nature of a geometric progression, as shown by the number of articles published in the field. The overwhelming majority of the articles are clinical in their presentation. The theoretic contributions are rather barren, and the preponderance of material is testimonial in nature. As one observes the entire field of treatment, there is no evidence that any school that has followed and developed a particular approach to psychotherapy continues to exist, and the adherents to a particular approach continue to cling to the concepts and techniques that they believe effective. While their loyalty is to be applauded, systematic research is in short supply.
>
> There is a plethora of techniques and maneuvers, all labeled as group psychotherapy. A conference held in 1972 put the following under the rubric of group psychotherapy: encounter, sensitivity training, Gestalt therapy, bioenergetics, family therapy, consciousness-raising, transactional analysis, interactional analysis, psychosynthesis, theatre of encounter, group games, movement in depth, fantasy imagery, alexander techniques, rolfing. In a conference held in 1980 additional terms such as conjoint therapy entered the group therapy vocabulary.

There is no conclusive evidence concerning the success of any group therapy method, whichever the theoretical premises they chose. Even more difficult, is assessing the degree of success with sociopaths. Following the literature (Agee, 1979; Allison & Harmala, 1981; Barnhill, 1980; Baron, 1977; Cleckley, 1976; Hamburg & Trudeau, 1981; Hare & Schalling, 1978; Hersov & Shaffer, 1978; Keith, 1984; Masterson, 1980; Mednick et al., 1986; Reid, 1978; Wolfgang, 1968; Wolman, 1973, 1983a, 1983b; and others), one must take a cautious attitude concerning the outcome of the various methods of treatments of sociopaths. It seems, however, that social, group-type approaches to treatment of antisocial individuals could achieve considerable success.

Lavin et al. (1984) conducted group therapy with antisocial, acting-out junior-high-school students, the average age 14, three boys and three girls and later five boys and three girls. The therapy was conducted on a junior-high-school campus in a special-education program. The therapists were a male psychiatrist and a female special-education teacher. The group therapy followed the "skill streaming model" (Goldstein et al., 1980) of role-playing in hypothetical situations that should prepare them to use their skills in real situations. The main task of the group was to foster social skills that would prepare the participants to relate to other people in a nonhostile and self-controlled manner. Time-out and point-system methods were used for disapproval of antisocial behavior and approval of proper behavior.

There have been attempts to modify antisocial behavior by group therapies (Julian & Killman, 1979). It seems that in all instances the degree of success depended more on the personality characteristics of the therapists than on the method they used. Sociopathic individuals try to manipulate anyone with whom they interact and show no respect for or cooperation with anyone they view as being a weak person. Firm, matter-of-fact, realistic and self-assured therapists have a better chance with them.

Group therapy with antisocial adolescents can hardly be successfully conducted on a voluntary basis. Some degree of restraint provided by a larger and authoritarian institution, such as a school, a hospital, or any other organization, can provide regular attendance at group sessions and give a chance for success. This rule of a larger authoritarian system applies also to adult group therapy settings.

COMPOSITION OF THERAPEUTIC GROUPS

In working with sociopaths, one should choose between a group composed exclusively of sociopathic individuals and a group of mixed clinical types with one or two sociopaths. It seems that mixed composition of a group is advisable in outpatient, voluntary treatment, whereas in institutional treatment, homogeneous group therapy is a better choice. The reasons are quite obvious. Acting-out, violent sociopaths do not seek psychotherapy; when they are hospitalized, jailed, or restrained in some way, they could be talked into or even forced to participate in group therapy. Any other clinical types and any other mental patients would have a difficult time in therapy group with acting-out, violent sociopaths. Thus, a monolithic group comprised of violent sociopaths would function better (see Chapter 19).

On the other hand, nonviolent sociopaths may willingly undergo psychotherapy. In most instances their willingness is not related to their antisocial, exploitative nature, but to hypochondriacal fears or paranoid suspicions directed to their family members or job or business associates. In such a case a mixed group composition gives a better chance for progress.

On several occasions I had one or two sociopathic young adults in a psychotherapeutic group comprised of six to eight individuals of diverse clinical types. I avoided clinically homogenous composition of groups; I believe that diverse clinical groups, males and females, have a better chance of interaction and can learn more from one another. An exceedingly selfish, self-centered, and self-righteous woman who was cheating on her husband and sleeping around, expecting little gifts, was shocked when a group member told her that she "whores away her marriage." Sociopaths would probably approve of her behavior, but the harsh comment made a dent in her attitude.

Sociopaths are usually intolerant, hostile, belligerent, and provoke conflicts. They tend to ascribe their own feelings and attitudes to others. Projections and paranoid accusations may become disruptive to the group process, and it is up to the therapist to interpret and disarm (Wolman, 1964). This would become difficult in a group comprised only of sociopaths, but a group with one or two sociopaths can exercise social pressure. Most sociopaths are sensitive to what other people think of them and crave approval for what they believe to be "innocent behavior." Group criticism, mollified and cautiously interpreted by the therapist, can be of some help in the therapist's work.

Apparently, compulsory participation in an institutional setting is the only method that promises some degree of therapeutic success. As already mentioned, success or lack of success in group psychotherapy with acting-out sociopathic adolescents depends on structural environment and on the personality of the therapists more than on the method they use. An active participation on the part of the therapist is a necessity, and the ability to tolerate provocative behavior is a prerequisite of success. A combination of understanding and firmness is usually the productive approach. The results of group therapy with adolescents are a mixed bag, and there is no uniform evidence of their success (Julian & Killman, 1979) but one must keep in mind the two most relevant ingredients: a strict, disciplinary environment and a firm and realistic therapist.

19

Residential Treatment

LEGAL ASPECTS

According to McCord and McCord (1964), psychotherapy of sociopaths "offers little hope but no assurance of success: ". . . Incarceration alone, while protecting society, does not seem to change basic personality trends." As mentioned earlier, sociopaths rarely feel the need for psychological treatment and don't have the slightest desire to change their life-style. They rarely blame themselves; they rarely, if ever, feel guilty, but frequently blame others.

Since sociopaths have little or no motivation for psychotherapeutic help, perhaps forced psychotherapy in a mental hospital or in a prison might do a little better. However, sociopaths try to take advantage of the situation of anyone who allows it, be it other inmates, other patients, nurses, or doctors. Sociopaths are usually very demanding and always ask for special privileges. In the university hospital where I taught and supervised residents in psychiatry, we had a few "mild" sociopaths who stole things from other patients and nurses, demanded special privileges, and frequently verbally and physically assaulted patients who could not defend themselves.

In a British study reported by Gibbens (1968), hospitalized sociopaths did not benefit much from hospital treatment; almost 60% of them were sentenced before and after their hospitalization. In another British study, Gunn (1975) concluded that forced treatment of sociopaths in psychiatric hospitals is counterproductive, for sociopaths need special treatment centers where they have to be treated according to the level of their violent behavior.

There have been several efforts to regulate the forced treatment of sociopaths, and a few will be mentioned below.

The Elizabethan Vagrancy Act of 1597 authorized forceful impressment for service in the Royal Navy of all "idle persons, rogues, vagabonds and sturdy beggars." Justices were requested to forcefully recruit them to years of compulsive service in the Royal Navy. There was no evidence of personality changes, nor was there any concern about psychological changes in these individuals.

In 1741 the British House of Commons passed the Act for the Speedy and Effectual Recruiting of His Majesty's Land Forces and Marines, which authorized the "impressment," that is, forceful inducing, of criminal and antisocial individuals. Most of them were sociopaths who joined the armed forces. The enlisted sociopaths acted in a violent and ruthless manner, stealing, robbing, and extorting money. There was a great deal of resentment from regular and voluntary servicemen against the "impressment," although many people believed that the "impressment" system freed the cities of Great Britain from undesirable elements. With the gradual improvement of conditions of service in the army and the navy and the growing public criticism against the forcible impressment, the entire system was abolished in 1859.

In 1925, the Dutch parliament issued a law that provides special legal provisions for the treatment of sociopaths. The law took effect in 1928. It has undergone several changes, but even today the results of the institutional treatment are quite controversial.

FORCED TREATMENT

Apparently, prisons are not very successful as therapeutic institutions, but no society could allow violent sociopaths to assault innocent people. Small wonder that almost all civilized nations have sought ways of combining forceful jail detention with some sort of psychological treatment. Mannheim (1981) addressed the Fourth International Congress of Criminology on Mentally Abnormal Offenders on the need to foster the offenders' adjustment to the moral and legal standards of the society. So far, a slight improvement has been noticed and the rate of recidivism has dropped in many forensic institutions.

A great deal of soul searching is going on in several countries concerning the psychiatric and psychological treatment of offenders, whatever their personality makeup.

The Model Sentencing Act of 1963 in the United States emphasizes that one offense is not a useful guide for sentencing and the evaluation of the offender rather than the offense should guide the sentencing judges. There have been several efforts to use both more lenient and more strict approaches in the treatment of acting-out, violent individuals, and the choice of methods is still quite controversial (Agee, 1979; Campbell, 1982; Dietz & Rada, 1982; Jones, 1984; Sandler, 1979; and many others).

At this point it seems necessary to draw a distinction between the treatment of sociopaths and that of other disturbed individuals, especially in regard to the use of forceful and punitive methods. It must be made clear that the fear of punishment could not stop a violent paranoid schizophrenic who acts under unconscious impulses. I had worked for years with hospitalized schizophrenics who physically attacked doctors and nurses, being driven by an irresistible urge. In lucid moments they explained that they heard voices ordering them to break the glass wall of the nurses' station, even when this caused serious physical harm to themselves. They experienced no fear when they tore the nurses' aprons or threw a cup of coffee in their faces or when they hit a doctor's head with a fist or a broomstick or badly wounded their fist by hitting a glass barrier. One schizophrenic patient set her house on fire and suffered heavy burns, but she felt that she did exactly what she was supposed to do. They were both aware and unaware of their actions, and their mental state resembled that of psychomotor epileptics who experience no fear. Their actions, whenever they are in a trance, are neither conscious nor unconscious. They are unaware of what they are doing nor are they asleep or in a somnambulic trance. I call this state of mind *protoconscious* (Wolman, 1986), that is, somewhat between being aware of what one is doing and unaware of the possible consequences. Thus, punitive methods are of no avail with schizophrenics or with psychomotor epileptics whose minds tend to become protoconscious.

Nothing of that kind goes on in the minds of sociopaths, unless they are heavy drinkers, drug addicts, or severely deteriorated. Sociopaths are fully aware of their actions and usually enjoy their selfish and/or aggressive behavior. Thus, the fear of being caught, punished, and hurt is the usual, if not the only, deterrent. One of my sociopathic female patients who hit her mother called me asking what to do and where to hide when her father came home and might beat her up. Sociopaths have no guilt feelings, but the fear of being hurt might act as a deterrent, and therefore strict disciplinary treatment could be of some value.

Crabtree and Douglas (1985) described the Regimental Inmate Discipline (RID) program conducted by the Oklahoma Department of Corrections. This program was developed as a result of the Specialized Offender Accountability Program devised in Oklahoma in November 1983 by the Department of Corrections. A few excerpts follow:

> Under the RID program, offenders actually begin their participation during the 90–120 day period that sentence recommendations to the courts are being developed. Partic-

ipants are subject to physical conditioning, rigid dress code, personal grooming and hygiene standards, limitations on personal property, structured leisure and recreation activities, rigid living area, cleanliness standards, early lockdown, minimized idleness, and intensive programming. In return, they are afforded the opportunity to influence—by appropriate behavior—the length of their sentences.

Since its inception in January 1984, the RID Unit has received 449 eligible offenders, with 158 of the more recently assigned offenders currently participating. Of those who have completed RID, 40 (13.7 percent) have been program failures and transferred to other Oklahoma institutions for extended incarceration. Fifty-two (20.7 percent) have been transferred in a positive direction to a minimum security facility for skill training or program participation prior to release; 64 (25.4 percent) have been transferred to a community treatment center for work release prior to release. Eighty-seven (34.6 percent) have been released directly to the streets under probation, with intensive supervision stipulations. (pp. 38–39)

Similar and different experiments are going on in the United States and in other countries. The reported results are far from being uniform, but it seems that a strict and structured environment treatment carries a hope for success. Some evidence to this effect was brought by several studies. One may say that, in general, better therapeutic results are obtained in structured and disciplined correctional institutions than in any outpatient settings (Goldstone, 1983; Hare, 1970, 1975; Robins, 1977).

HOSPITAL AND INSTITUTIONAL TREATMENT

Apparently, treatment of aggressive, violent children, adolescents, and adults is exceedingly difficult and often futile (McCarthy, 1978; Pfeffer, 1980). Hospitalization might be the necessary step that prevents additional acts of violence; it may also enable one to establish some degree of control unavailable in outpatient and private office practice. The unruly, provocative, and hostile behavior does not contribute to the development of positive transference to the therapist, and it may prevent any therapeutic progress.

Many years ago, I was director of a sleep-in institution for disturbed children and adolescents; half of them were sociopaths. The sociopathic youngsters were referred by private practitioners unable to handle the frequent outbursts of negative transference and overt hostility. The institutional setting, with established patterns of behavior, such as getting up on time, rigid hours of meals, supervised teaching and occupational hours, and strictly organized group and individual therapy sessions, gave the youngsters the feeling that someone cares, is concerned with their well-being, and is determined to help them. They had become aware of the inadequate relationship with their wishy-washy, uncaring, and sometimes hostile parents, and of our staff's devoted and no-nonsense attitude. However, in many instances, our results were rather unsatisfactory. The big plus was the strict discipline and the no-nonsense, matter-of-fact, realistic approach of our staff, but we definitely failed in some cases for reasons that are not too clear. Some of the older adolescents, boys and girls, would not trust us and believed that we, like everyone else in the world, only pretended to be fair and friendly.

Treatment of sociopaths in a hospital setting is more promising than outpatient and prison therapy, but there is no evidence of 100% success in any setting. There are several distinct approaches to hospital treatment in general and to hospital treatment of sociopaths in particular (Carney, 1978; Dietz & Rada, 1982; Jones, 1984; Schwartz et al., 1983). At the present time there is a tendency for dehospitalization of mental patients, and many of them are prematurely discharged to some sort of "community" arrangement that is in many instances poorly equipped, inadequately staffed, and not always prepared to offer the care the patients need.

The present status of hospitals has been described by Schwartz et al. (1983, pp. 276–277) as follows:

> Until recent years psychiatric hospitals were considered to be the most traditional and stable setting for the care of the mentally ill. Today the field of hospital care is in ferment.

Basic issues (e.g., what is psychiatric illness, who is sick, who needs hospitalization, what is good hospital care, who is capable of treating mentally ill patients, what is recovery, when should a patient be discharged) have become hotly debated and remain unresolved. The continuum of opinion ranges from those people who feel that hospitalization should be avoided whenever not absolutely necessary to those who feel that prolonged hospitalization offers a patient the best possibility for restructuring his personality and recovering from his illness. Scarce resources, time limits dictated by third-party payments and the need to provide care for large numbers of patients have required innovative solutions and procedures. Hospital treatment today includes crisis intervention units, intensive milieu units with emphasis on group interaction, behavior modification wards, day hospitals and long-term settings with emphasis on individual psychotherapy. Newly available are a host of biologic diagnostic and therapeutic interventions that in the decade to come may be expected to add precision to the care of the psychiatric patient. Within each setting, hospitals vary according to who treats patients, with what modality of treatment and according to which theoretical framework. In some settings only psychiatrists do traditional psychotherapy, whereas in others members of other disciplines or generic mental health workers are the therapist of record. In large cities, mental health workers with little formal training but with knowledge of the patients' cultural origins and familiarity with the patients' language, are often called upon to take major treatment responsibilities. Such trends are upsetting to some professionals, welcomed by others and a matter of indifference to a third group who believe that medication and removal of the patient from his conflictual environment are all that can be accomplished in a hospitalization, especially a brief one.

Within this social climate several efforts are going on aimed at providing rational help to sociopathic children, adolescents, and adults. The success of these efforts greatly depends on the level of structured and disciplined environment as well as on the unconditionally supportive and caring attitude of the therapist and the hospital staff. One of the difficulties in the treatment of antisocial individuals is related to the personality of the therapist. Eissler (1950) stressed the therapist's resistance as follows: "In order to understand the delinquent, one must temporarily relinquish one's own moral standards . . . and since these are a recent acquisition . . . the treatment of some delinquents is doomed to failure by the therapist's own resistance" (p. 121).

Hospital treatment of sociopaths uses all available methods, including neuropharmacology, group therapy, family therapy, and the various psychotherapeutic techniques. Sociopaths have little self-confidence and self-esteem, and most of them tend to be defensively or offensively belligerent. Many of them tend to act out their aggressive behavior against the hospital environment, and a slight provocation can elicit violence. Moreover, outside control of their aggressive behavior and even some degree of self-control gained by treatment may lead to redirecting of their hostility toward themselves and produce depression. In many instances, the outside or inside control of aggression leads to a series of psychosomatic symptoms.

Sociopathic adolescents with poor impulse control (the "incorrigible" aggressive adolescents) are the "most difficult to manage" (Jones, 1984, p. 359). The treatment of sociopathic acting-out adolescents requires a permanent, secure, and psychologically committed environment in the hospital, in the community, and in their families.

> Collaboration among the hospital, the community system of stepdown services, and the family is crucial to the success of psychiatric hospital treatment. In order to have an effective milieu, and thus achieve positive therapeutic results, the hospital ward must be utilized as a dynamic component of a continuum of services. A coordinated utilization of this continuum of stepdown services prepares the adolescent to cope in a more adaptive manner to a less restrictive therapeutic environment and, eventually, to his permanent residence where his "psychological taproot" is located. It may be necessary for a case manager to be the adolescent's advocate and provide continuity of care as he moves through the various stepdown facilities. Ideally, the case manager would have the knowledge and skills of a psychiatric social

worker. The case manager would provide the "glue" that keeps the team focused on the treatment process, and would coordinate the many members of the extended treatment team and collaborate with the involved community agencies. (*ibid.*, p. 363)

It is tempting for the hospital staff to react aggressively to aggressive sociopaths and use overpowering aggressive methods in order to control the acting-out sociopaths. It is not easy to retain persistent calmness and explain to the patient that the hospital staff is here to help him or her and acting-out disrupts the process of treatment and is counterproductive.

According to Jones (1984, pp. 368–369):

> The violent, aggressive patient who is dangerous to others will profit initially from a simplified milieu that keeps him safe by the use of containment. As this containment is maintained and violence recedes, the adolescent will become more anxious and depressed. Staff members must be patient and supportively encouraging toward the adolescent at this time. Like an overwhelmed infant, the adolescent's violent panic requires a "supportive shield" to assist him to feel safe and secure, as a good mother cares for her child in a concerned, caring, protective milieu. These two therapeutic milieu techniques, containment and support, must be administered together in order to reduce the frequency and degree of the youth's panic reactions. Because each panic reaction depletes and weakens the ego, techniques that help an adolescent cope without panic-rage reactions are eventually ego strengthening.
>
> As the adolescent improves and copes without destructive aggression, he or she emerges from the ongoing need for containment and support. At this time, the aggressive adolescent needs to learn social skills. The next milieu technique, the therapeutic use of structures, can provide a predictable treatment setting.
>
> As the aggressive adolescent's ego becomes even stronger, the milieu technique of involvement begins to be the patient's main therapeutic environmental interaction on the ward. In this phase of milieu therapy, the adolescent often learns about how his or her behavior affects other people. The

patient becomes sensitive to interpersonal relationships and to the potential constructive or destructive influences others may have on him or her. Involvement helps the patient to develop insight, judgment, and the ability to recognize the more complicated aspects of interpersonal relationships.

20

The Road to Life

There is also another, rarely used method in treatment of sociopathic individuals, especially adolescents and young adults. The way this method is used in fostering violent behavior offers a clue and a possible direction of control and treatment of violence. Apparently, human energies cannot remain idle; they must be used in a constructive or a destructive manner.

The key word is *purpose*. Human behavior tends to be goal-directed. All terrorist groups give their members the sense of purpose. The leaders tell their followers that the violent acts serve an important goal, and they are not juvenile pranks or savage cruelties, but they are acted out in the name of a lofty slogan, be it religious, national, or sociopolitical.

Obviously, well-adjusted adolescents and adults may subscribe to these ideas, but they would not join the terrorists and their criminal actions. One could not say that all members of terrorist gangs are sociopaths or paranoid schizophrenics, but many of the leaders apparently are fanatic, paranoid schizophrenics, and many of the followers are sociopaths who found an easy excuse for their antisocial psychological urge—that is, the need for power at the expense of other human beings.

The treatment of sociopaths should go in an opposite direction. One should give the feeling of *constructive power* and help them find satisfaction in behavior directed toward positive goals, be it religious, political, national, or any other.

Power can be used in two directions: positive and negative, to satisfy human needs and to prevent their satisfaction, to create and to demolish, to protect life and to destroy it. Undoubtedly, it is much easier to destroy than to build, to demolish than to create. The building of a magnificent architectonic structure and painting of a masterpiece requires great creative abilities and a tremendous amount of work, but one little match can destroy the greatest painting and one incendiary bomb can demolish the most beautiful building. People who have little power and are aware of their weakness may be prone to embark on the negative and easy way of showing power they don't possess. The less power one possesses and/or the more one doubts one's own power, the more one is inclined to assert oneself by resorting to violence. Adolescents who are aware of the fact that they are not yet adults are more inclined toward the use of negative power than adults who are capable of finding more positive outlets. The Biblical Cain probably felt outdistanced by his younger brother; being unable to outdo Abel, he killed him. The Roman Romulus, who started to build a new city out of nowhere, was not too sure about his ability to retain law and order in his domain, and he killed his brother Remus, who transgressed his orders.

Insecurity and aggression are Siamese twins. The fear of death common to all living nature is the main source of anxiety in human beings. Strivings for self-aggrandizement, for material possessions, and for glory are the positive aspects of the futile human craving for absolute power and immortality. Unfortunately, there is much more on the negative side than on the positive side of that striving: envy, competition, jealousy, paranoid fear of true and imaginary enemies, morbid anticipation of catastrophes, and self-fulfilling prophecies of wars, all are daily occurrences at all times.

In clinical practice, one comes across several cases of overt and covert inclination toward violent acts. Most violent acts are committed by people who suffer a severe feeling of inferiority, rejection, and paranoid delusions of persecution. People who feel secure do not expect everybody to love them, and they can take in stride the inevitable ups and downs of human fortune. Immature and insecure individuals, and especially sociopaths, are less capable of accepting frustration and rejection and are more prone to aggression in alleged self-defense. Sociopathic individuals (the hyperinstrumental, narcissistic types) are more inclined toward antisocial behavior than any other clinical group. Most of them believe that they are innocent victims of injustice and they have to defend themselves against a cold and hostile world. When they perpetuate a crime, they believe that they were justified to do whatever they did. Most sociopaths I treated in private practice and in hospitals maintained that their victims were guilty and they were provoked to act in self-defense.

Many acts of violence are committed by people in a mob or in a gang. The mob psychology weakens individual superegos and is often inspired by a morbid and malicious leader. The awareness of consequences is substantially reduced and the "security in numbers" may create the feeling of unlimited power leading to unpunishable acts. Ultrapermissive and pseudoliberal contemporary attitudes greatly contribute to a sociopathic psychology in our cities and is therefore, at least, partly to be blamed for the increase of violence. The feeling that one can get away with murder destroys one's reality principle and facilitates a mass regression into id-driven, acting-out behavior.

Psychotherapy of sociopaths should be directed toward a productive utilization of one's physical and mental resources. As mentioned above, human energy cannot stay idle for too long; it can be used productively or destructively, and it is up to the therapist in clinical cases and to public leaders in society at large to direct these forces into positive and constructive channels. Immediately after the Soviet Revolution, hundreds of thousands of wayward youths were roaming the streets of Russia, robbing, mugging, and murdering innocent victims. Makarenko (1951), in his beautiful book *The Road to Life*, described how the *bezprizornye* had been inspired by the goal of rebuilding the ruins of Russia. Constructive guidance redirected their energies into a great heroic effort for the well-being of the society and for their own mental health.

Therapy is not enough. The cure of sociopaths requires a much greater effort. Sociopathy is more a sociocultural problem than a clinical problem. The mushrooming of various types of antisocial sociopathic behavior, be it public corruption or petty burglary, street mugging or terrorist gangs, requires a concentrated public effort directed toward giving young people positive and worthwhile moral purposes of life.

Bibliography

Agee, V. L. *Treatment of the violent incorrigible adolescent.* Lexington, MA: Heath, 1979.

Aichhorn, A. *Wayward youth.* New York: Viking, 1935.

Alexander, F. and French, T. M. *Psychoanalytic psychotherapy.* New York: Ronald, 1946.

Alexander, F. & Healy, W. *Roots of crime: Psychoanalytic studies.* New York: Knopf, 1935.

Allison, J. Clinical contributions of the Wechsler Adult Intelligence Scale. In B. B. Wolman (Ed.), *Clinical diagnosis of mental disorders: A handbook.* New York: Plenum Press, 1978, pp. 355–392.

Allison, D. & Harmala, W. 110 murderers in a psychiatric hospital. *Journal of Forensic Psychiatry,* 1981, 3, 37–40.

American Psychiatric Association. *A psychiatric glossary: The meaning of words most frequently used in psychiatry.* Washington, DC: American Psychiatric Association, 1957.

American Psychiatric Association. *Diagnostic and Statistical Manual of mental disorder: DSM III* (3rd ed.), Washington, DC: American Psychiatric Association, 1980.

Anchor, K. N. & Cross, H. J. Maladaptive aggression, moral perspectives and socialization process. *Journal of Personality and Social Psychology,* 1974, 30, 163–168.

Andry, R. G. Parental affection and delinquency. In M. E. Wolfgang, L. Sevitz, & N. Johnston (Eds.), *Sociology of crime and delinquency.* New York: Macmillan, 1962.

Bandura, A. *Principles of behavior modification.* New York: Holt, Rinehart and Winston, 1969.

Bandura, A. *Aggression: A social learning analysis.* Englewood Cliffs, NJ: Prentice-Hall, 1973.
Bandura, A., Ross, D., & Ross, S. Transmission of aggression through imitation of aggressive models. *Journal of Abnormal and Social Psychology,* 1961, 63, 311–318.
Bandura, A., Ross, D., & Ross, A. Imitation of film-mediated aggressive models. *Journal of Abnormal and Social Psychology,* 1963, 66, 3–11.
Bandura, A. & Walters, R. H. *Adolescent aggression.* New York: Ronald, 1959.
Barnhill, L. Basic interventions for violence in families. *Hospital and Community Psychiatry,* 1980, 31, 219–225.
Baron, R. *Human aggression.* New York: Plenum, 1977.
Barron, M. L. *The juvenile in a delinquent society.* New York: Knopf, 1954.
Bender, L. Psychopathic behavior disorders in children. In R. M. Lindner & R. V. Seliger (Eds.), *Handbook of correctional psychology.* New York: Philosophical Library, 1947, pp. 360–377.
Berkowitz, L. *Aggression: A social-psychological analysis.* New York: McGraw-Hill, 1962.
Berman, S. Antisocial character disorder: Its etiology and relationship to delinquency. *American Journal of Orthopsychiatry,* 1959, 29, 612–621.
Bowlby, J. *Maternal care and mental health.* Geneva: World Health Organization, 1952.
Brown, G. L. & Goodwin, F. K. Aggression, adolescence and psychobiology. In C. R. Keith (Ed.), *The aggressive adolescent.* New York: Free Press, 1984.
Brown, G. L., Ballenger, J. C., Minochiello, M. D., & Goodwin, F. K. Human aggression and its relationship to cerebrospinal fluid. In M. Sandler (Ed.), *Psychopharmacology of aggression.* New York: Raven, 1979, pp. 131–148.
Callahan, E. J. & Leitenberg, H. Aversion therapy for sexual deviation. *Journal of Abnormal Psychology,* 1973, 81, 60–73.
Campbell, M. Drugs in aggressive behavior. *Journal of the American Academy of Child Psychiatry,* 1982, 21, 107–117.
Carney, F. L. Outpatient treatment of an aggressive offender. *American Journal of Psychotherapy,* 1977, 31, 265–274.
Carney, F. L. Inpatient treatment programs. In W. H. Reid (Ed.), *The psychopath.* New York: Brunner/Mazel, 1978, pp. 261–300.
Cazeneuve, J. *Les rites et la condition humaine.* Paris: Presses Universitaires, 1958.
Christiansen, K. O. Recidivism among collaborators—A follow-up study of 2946 Danish men convicted of collaboration with the Germans during World War II. In M. G. Wolfgang (Ed.), *Crime and culture.* New York: Wiley, 1968, pp. 245–283.
Chwast, J. Sociopathic behavior in children. In B. B. Wolman (Ed.), *Manual of child psychopathology.* New York: McGraw-Hill, 1972, pp. 436–445.
Cleckley, H. *The mask of sanity.* (5th ed.) St. Louis: Mosby, 1976.
Cohen, A. K. *Delinquent boys: The culture of the gang.* Glencoe, IL: Free Press, 1955.
Crabtree, L. & Douglas, P. Military discipline: Young offenders learn accountability. *Corrections Today,* 1985, 8, 38–39.
Crain, W. C. & Smoke, L. Rorschach aggressive content in normal and problematic children. *Journal of Personality Assessment,* 1981, 45, 2–4.

Crowe, R. R. An adoption study of antisocial personality. *Archives of General Psychiatry*, 1974, *31*, 785–791.
Crowe, R. R. Adoption studies in psychiatry. *Biological Psychiatry*, 1975, *10*, 353–371.
Curry, J. F. & Thompson, R. J. Jr. Patterns of behavioral disturbance in developmentally disturbed children. *Journal of Pediatric Psychology*, 1982, *7*, 61–73.
Dalmau, C. J. Psychopathy and psychopathic behavior: A psychoanalytic approach. *Archives of Criminal Psychodynamics*, 1961, *4*, 443–455.
Dietz, P. E. & Rada, R. T. Risks and benefits of working with violent patients. *Psychiatric Annals*, 1982, *12*, 502–508.
Dollard, J., Miller, N. E., Doob, L. W., Mowrer, O. H., & Sears, R. R. *Frustration and aggression*. New Haven, CT: Yale University Press, 1939.
Eichelman, B., Elliott, G., & Barchas, S. Biochemical, pharmacological and genetic aspects of aggression. In D. Hamburg & M. Trudeau (Eds.), *Biobehavioral aspects of aggression*. New York: Liss, 1981, pp. 51–84.
Eissler, K. (Ed.), *Searchlights on delinquency*. New York: International Universities Press, 1949.
Eissler, K. R. Ego-psychological implications of the psychoanalytic treatment of delinquents. *Psychoanalytic Study of the Child*, 1950, *5*, 97–121.
Epstein, E. The self-concept of the delinquent female, *Smith College Studies in Social Work*, 1962, *32*, 220–234.
Erikson, M. L. & Embey, L. T. Class position, peers and delinquency. *Sociology and Social Research*, 1965, *49*, 268–282.
Eron, L. D. Prescription for reduction of aggression. *American Psychologist*, 1980, *35*, 244–252.
Eysenck, H. J. *Crime and personality*. London: Methuen, 1964.
Fields, W. S. & Sweet, W. H. (Eds.). *Neural bases of violence and aggression*. St. Louis: W. H. Green, 1975.
Fookes, B. H. Some experiences in the use of aversion therapy in male homosexuality, exhibitionism, and fetishism-transvestism. *British Journal of Psychiatry*, 1969, *115*, 339–341.
Frank, S. & Quinlan, D.M. Ego development and female delinquency. *Journal of Abnormal Psychology*, 1976, *85*, 505–510.
Freedman, A. M., Kaplan, H. I., & Sadock, B. J. (Eds.). *Comprehensive handbook of psychiatry* (2nd ed.) Baltimore, MD: Williams & Wilkins, 1975.
Freud, A. Certain types and stages of social maladjustment. In K. R. Eissler (Ed.), *Searchlights on delinquency*. New York: International Universities Press, 1949, pp. 193–204.
Friedlander, K. Latent delinquency and ego development. In K. R. Eissler (Ed.), *Searchlights on delinquency*. New York: International Universities Press, 1949, 205–215.
Galle, O. R., Gove, W. R., & McPherson, J. M. Population density and pathology. *Science*, 1972, *176*, 23–30.
Gant, B., Barnard, J., Kuhn, F., Jones, H., & Christophersen, E. A behaviorally based approach for improving intrafamilial communication patterns. *Journal of Clinical Child Psychology*, 1981, *10*, 102–106.
Gibbens, T. C. N. Problems of clinical criminology. In M. E. Wolfgang (Ed.), *Crime and culture*. New York: Wiley, 1968, pp. 111–130.

Glover, E. *The roots of crime.* New York: International Universities Press, 1960.
Glueck, S. & Glueck, E. *Physique and delinquency.* New York: Harper, 1956.
Glueck, S. & Glueck, E. *Predicting delinquency and crime.* Cambridge, MA: Harvard University Press, 1959.
Glueck, S. & Glueck, E. *Family environment in delinquency.* Boston: Houghton Mifflin, 1962.
Goldstein, A., Spralkin, R., Gersha, N., & Klein, P. *Skillstreaming the adolescent.* Champaign, IL: Research Press, 1980.
Goldstone, S. The treatment of antisocial behavior. In B. B. Wolman (Ed.), *The therapist's handbook* (2nd ed.) New York: Van Nostrand Reinhold, 1983, pp. 463–482.
Graham, J. R. Minnesota Multiphasic Personality Inventory (MMPI). In B. B. Wolman (Ed.), *Clinical diagnosis of mental disorders.* New York: Plenum, 1978, pp. 311–331.
Greenacre, P. Conscience in the psychopath. *American Journal of Orthopsychiatry,* 1945, 15, 495–509.
Gualtieri, C. T., Barnill, J., McGimsey, J., & Schell, D. Tardive dyskinesia and other movement disorders in children treated with psychotropic drugs. *Journal of the American Academy of Child Psychiatry,* 1980, 19, 491–510.
Gunn, J. Forensic psychiatry and psychopathic patients. *British Journal of Psychiatry,* 1975, 9, 302–307.
Hamburg, D. A., & Trudeau, M. (Eds.) *Biobehavioral aspects of aggression.* New York: Liss, 1981.
Hardman, D. G. Historical perspectives of gang research. *Journal of Research in Crime and Delinquency,* 1967, 4, 5–28.
Hare, R. D. *Psychopathy: Theory and research.* New York: Wiley, 1970.
Hare, R. D. Psychopathy. In P. Venables & S. M. Christie (Eds.), *Psychophysiology.* New York: Wiley, 1975.
Hare, R. D. & Schalling, D. (Eds.). Psychopathic behavior: *Approaches to research.* New York: Wiley, 1978.
Hathaway, S. R. & Monachesi, E. D. (Eds.). *Analyzing and predicting juvenile delinquency with the MMPI.* Minneapolis: University of Minnesota Press, 1953.
Healy, W. & Bronner, A. *New lights on delinquency and its treatment.* New Haven, CT: Yale University Press, 1936.
Hersov, L. A. & Shaffer, D. (Eds.) *Aggression and antisocial behavior in childhood and adolescence.* Oxford: Pergamon, 1978.
Hoffman, L., Rosen, S., & Lippitt, R. Parental coerciveness, child autonomy and child's role in school. *Sociometry,* 1960, 23, 11–18.
Huesmann, L. R., Lefkowitz, M. M., & Eron, L. D. Sum of MMPI scales F, 4, and Q as a measure of aggression. *Journal of Consulting and Clinical Psychology,* 1978, 46, 1071–1078.
Johnson, A. Juvenile delinquency. In S. Arieti (Ed.), *Handbook of psychiatry.* New York: Basic Books, 1959.
Jones, J. D. Principles of hospital treatment of the aggressive adolescent. In C. R. Keith (Ed.), *The aggressive adolescent.* New York: Free Press, 1984, pp. 359–402.
Julian, A. & Killman, P. Group treatment of juvenile delinquents: A review of

the outcome literature. *International Journal of Group Psychotherapy*, 1979, 29, 3–37.
Karpman, B. The myth of psychopathic personality. *American Journal of Psychiatry*, 1948, 104, 523–534.
Karpman, B. (Ed.). *Symposia on child and juvenile delinquency.* Washington, DC: Psychodynamic Monographs, 1959.
Keith, C. R. (Ed.). *The aggresssive adolescent.* New York: Free Press, 1984.
Kempler, H. L. & Scott, V. Can systematically scored thematic stories reflect the attributes of the antisocial child syndrome? *Journal of Projective Techniques and Personality Assessment*, 1970, 34, 204–211.
Kernberg, P. F. Counterindication to adolescent psychoanalysis. In B.B. Wolman (Ed.), *International encyclopedia of psychiatry, psychology, psychoanalysis and neurology.* New York: Aesculapius, 1977, Vol. 3, pp. 400–403.
Kohlberg, L., LaCrosse, J., & Ricks, D. The predictability of adult mental health from childhood behavior. In B. B. Wolman (Ed.), *Manual of child psychopathology.* New York: McGraw-Hill, 1972, pp. 1217–1284.
Kostowski, W., Pucilowski, O., & Plazmik, A. Effect of stimulation of brain serotonergic system on mousekilling behavior in rats. *Physiology and Behavior*, 1980, 25, 161–165.
Krauss, B. J. & Krauss, H. H. Sociopaths: Wolman's view. In B. B. Wolman (Ed.), *International encyclopedia of psychiatry, psychology, psychoanalysis and neurology.* New York: Aesculapius, 1977, Vol. 10, pp. 363–364.
Lavin, G. K., Trabka, S., & Kahn, E. M. Group therapy with aggressive and delinquent adolescents. In C. R. Keith (Ed.), *The aggressive adolescent.* New York: Free Press, 1984, pp. 240–267.
Lazarus, A. A., & Fay, A. Resistance or rationalization? A cognitive-behavioral perspective. In P. L. Wachtel (Ed.), *Resistance: Psychodynamic and behavioral approaches.* New York: Plenum, 1982.
Lefkowtiz, M. M., Eron, L. D., Walder, L. O., & Huesmann, L. R. *Growing up to be violent.* Elmsford, NY: Pergamon, 1977.
Leventhal, B. L. The neuropharmacology of violent and aggressive behavior in children and adolescents. In C. R. Keith (Ed.), *The aggressive adolescent.* New York: Free Press, 1984, pp. 299–358.
Levy, D. M. The deprived and indulged forms of psychopathic personality. *American Journal of Orthopsychiatry*, 1951, 21, 250–254.
Lion, J. R. (Ed.). *Personality disorders.* Baltimore, MD: Williams & Wilkins, 1974.
Lippman, H. S. The "psychopathic personality" in childhood. In B. Karpman (Ed.), *Symposia on child and juvenile delinquency.* Washington, DC: Psychodynamic Monographs, 1959, pp. 4–8.
Lochman, J. E., Nelson, W. M., & Sims, J. P. A cognitive behavioral program for use with aggressive children. *Journal of Clinical Psychology*, 1980, 10, 146–148.
Lombroso, C. *Crime, its causes and remedies.* Boston: Little, Brown, 1911.
Loney, J., Langhome, J. E., & Paternite, C. E. An empirical basis for subgrouping the hyperkinetic/minimal brain dysfunction syndrome. *Journal of Abnormal Psychology*, 1978, 87, 431–441.
Lowrey, L. G. The develoment of psychopathic reactions. *American Journal of Orthopsychiatry*, 1951, 21, 242–249.

Maj, J., Mogilnicka, E., & Korolecka-Magiera, A. Effects of chronic administration of anti-depressant drugs on aggressive behavior induced by clonidine in mice. *Pharmacology, Biochemistry and Behavior*, 1980, *15*, 153–154.

Makarenko, A. S. *The road to life—An epic in education*. Moscow: Foreign Languages Publishing House, 1951.

Mannheim, H. The criminal law and mentally abnormal offenders. *British Journal of Criminology*, 1981, *1*, 203–220.

Mark, V. H. & Erwin, F. R. *Violence and the brain*. New York: Harper and Row, 1970.

Marshall, T., & Mason, A. A framework for the analysis of juvenile delinquency analysis. *British Journal of Sociology*, 1968, *19*, 130–142.

Masterson, J. F. *From borderline adolescent to functioning adult*. New York: Brunner/Mazel, 1980.

McCarthy, J. Narcissism and the self in homicidal adolescents. *American Journal of Psychoanalysis*, 1978, *38*, 19–29.

McCord, W. & McCord, E. *Psychopathy and delinquency*. New York: Grune & Stratton, 1956.

McCord, W. & McCord, J. *The psychopath: An essay on the criminal mind*. New York: Van Nostrand Reinhold, 1964.

McCord, W., McCord, J., & Zola, I. K. *Origins of crime*. New York: Columbia University Press, 1959.

Mednick, S. A. & Christiansen, K. O. (Eds.). *Biosocial bases of criminality*. New York: Gardner, 1980.

Mednick, S. A. & Hutchings, B. Genetic and psychophysiological factors in asocial behavior. *Journal of the American Academy of Child Psychiatry*, 1978, *17*, 209–223.

Mednick, S. A., Schulsinger, J. T., Higgins, B., & Bell, R. A. (Eds.). *Genetics, environment and psychopathology*. Amsterdam: North Holland Publishing, 1986.

Mendelson, J. H. Endocrines and aggression. *Psychopharmacology Bulletin*, 1977, *13*, 22–23.

Monaha, J. *Predicting violent behavior*. New York: Sage Publication, 1981.

Monroe, R. R. *Brain dysfunction in aggressive criminals*. Lexington, MA: Lexington Books, 1978.

Morrison, H. L. The asocial child: A destiny or sociopathy? In W. H. Reid (Ed.), *The psychopath*. New York: Brunner/Mazel, 1978.

Mosher, D. L., O'Grady, K. E., & Katz, H. A. Hostility, guilt, guilt over aggression and self-punishment. *Journal of Personality Assessment*, 1980, *44*, 34–40.

Moss, G. R. & Rick, G. R. Overview: Applications of operant technology to behavioral disorders of adolescents. *American Journal of Psychiatry*, 1981, *138*, 1161–1169.

Moyers, K. E. *Physiology of aggression and implication for control*. New York: Raven Press, 1976.

Myerhoff, W. L. & Myerhoff, R.G. Field observations of middle-class "gangs." *Social Forces*, 1964, *42*, 328–336.

O'Neal, P., Robins, L. N., King, L. J., & Schaefer, J. Parental deviance and the genesis of sociopathic personality. *American Journal of Psychiatry*, 1962, *118*, 1114–1124.

Parker, T. & Allerton, R. *The courage of his convictions.* London: Hutchinson, 1962.
Patterson, G. *Families: Application of social learning to family life.* Champaign, IL: Research Press, 1975.
Pfeffer, C. Psychiatric hospital treatment of assaultive homicidal children. *American Journal of Psychotherapy*, 1980, 22, 197–207.
Pincus, J. H. Violence and epilepsy. *New England Journal of Medicine*, 1981, 305, 696–698.
Pribram, K. Comparative neurology and evolutions of behavior. In A. Roe & G. G. Simpson (Eds.), *Behavior and evolution.* New Haven, CT: Yale University Press, 1958.
Pritchard, J. C. *Treatise on insanity.* London: Gilbert and Piper, 1835.
Rada, R. T. (Ed.). *Clinical aspects of the rapist.* New York: Grune & Stratton, 1978.
Rampling, D. Aggression: A paradoxical response to trycyclic antidepressants. *American Journal of Psychiatry*, 1978, 135, 117–118.
Ransford, H. E. Isolation, powerlessness and violence. *American Journal of Sociology*, 1968, 73, 581–591.
Redl, F. & Wineman, D. *The aggressive child.* Glencoe, IL: Free Press, 1957.
Reid, W. H. (Ed.). *The psychopath: A comprehensive study of antisocial disorders and behaviors.* New York: Brunner/Mazel, 1978.
Rexford, E. N. (Ed.). *A developmental approach to problems of acting out.* New York: International University Press, 1978.
Robin, A. A controlled evaluation of problem-solving communication training with parent-adolescent conflict. *Behavior Therapy*, 1981, 12, 593–609.
Robins, E. Sociopathy. In B. B. Wolman (Ed.), *International encyclopedia of psychiatry, psychology, psychoanalysis and neurology.* New York: Aesculapius, 1977, Vol. 10, pp. 364–368.
Robins, L. N. *Deviant children grown up. A sociological and psychiatric study of sociopathic personality.* Huntington, NY: Krieger, 1974.
Robinson, S. M. *Juvenile delinquency.* New York: Holt Rinehart and Winston, 1965.
Rosenbaum, M. Group psychotherapies. In B. B. Wolman (Ed.), *The therapist's handbook* (2nd ed.) New York: Van Nostrand Reinhold, 1983, pp. 222–250.
Ross, A. O. *Child behavior therapy.* New York: Wiley, 1980.
Rugg, H. O. *Foundations for American education.* Yonkers, NY: World, 1947.
Sadoff, R. L. (Ed.). *Violence and responsibility: The individual, family and society.* New York: Medical and Scientific Books, 1978.
Sandler, M. (Ed.). *Psychopharmacology of aggression.* New York: Raven Press, 1979.
Schmideberg, M. Psychotherapy of the criminal psychopath. *Archives of Criminal Psychodynamics*, 1961, 4, 724–735.
Schreier, H. Use of propranolol in the treatment of post-encephalitic psychosis. *American Journal of Psychiatry*, 1979, 136, 840–841.
Schulsinger, F. Psychopathy: Heredity and environment. *International Journal of Mental Health*, 1972, 1, 190–206.
Schwartz, A. H., Perlman, B. B., & Swartzburg, M. Hospital care. In B. B.

Wolman (Ed.), *The therapist's handbook* (2nd ed.) New York: Van Nostrand Reinhold, 1983, pp. 251–282.

Scott, J. P. & Fredericson, E. The causes of fighting in mice and rats. *Physiological Zoology*, 1951, 24, 273–309.

Sears, R. R., Macoby, E. E., & Levin, H. *Patterns of child rearing*. New York: Harper and Row, 1957.

Shapiro, D. *Neurotic styles*. New York: Basic Books, 1965.

Smith, C., Alexander, P., Halatyn, T., & Roberts, C. *Report of the National Juvenile Justice Assessment Center*. Washington, DC: US Department of Justice, 1980.

Sorrels, J. Jr. What can be done about juvenile homicide? *Crime and Delinquency*, 1980, 18, 152–161.

Spergel, I. *Street gang work*. Garden City, NY: Doubleday, 1967.

Spitz, R. A. Possible infantile precursors of psychopathy. *American Journal of Orthopsychiatry*, 1959, 20, 240–248.

Stanfield, R. E. The interaction of family variables and gang variables in the etiology of delinquency. *Social Problems*, 1966, 13, 411–417.

Sullivan, H. S. *The interpersonal theory of psychiatry*. New York: Norton, 1953.

Tharp, R. G., & Wetzel, R. J. *Behavior modification in the natural environment*. New York: Academic Press, 1969.

Thrasher, F. *The gang*. Chicago: University of Chicago Press, 1930.

Tinklenberg, J. & Ochberg, F. M. Patterns of adolescent violence. In D. Hamburg & M. Trudeau (Eds.), *Biobehavioral aspects of aggression*. New York: Liss, 1981.

Valzelli, L. *Psychobiology of aggression and violence*. New York: Raven Press, 1981.

Vaz, E. D. (Ed.). *Middle class juvenile delinquency*. New York: Harper and Row, 1967.

Weathers, L. & Liberman, R. Contingency contracting with families of delinquent adolescents. *Behavior Therapy*, 1975, 6, 356–366.

Weinstock, M. & Weiss, C. Antagonism by propranolol of isolation induced aggression in mice. *Neuropharmacology*, 1980, 13, 653–656.

Weisfeld, G. E. The nature-nurture issue and the integrating concept of function. In B. B. Wolman (Ed.), *Handbook of developmental psychology*. Englewood Cliffs, NJ: Prentice-Hall, 1982, pp. 208–229.

Whyte, W. F. *Street corner society*. Chicago: University of Chicago Press, 1943.

Williams, D. T., Mehl, R., Yudofsky, S., Adams, D., & Rosenman, R. The efficacy of propranolol in uncontrolled rage outbursts in children and adolescents with organic brain dysfunction. *Journal of the American Academy of Child Psychiatry*, 1982, 21, 21–24.

Wilson, G. T. & Lazarus, A. A. Behavior modification and therapy. In B. B. Wolman (Ed.), *The therapist's handbook* (2nd ed.) New York: Van Nostrand Reinhold, 1983, pp. 121–154.

Wilson, G. T. & O'Leary, K. D. *Principles of behavior therapy*. Englewood Cliffs, NJ: Prentice-Hall, 1980.

Wilson, H. Juvenile delinquency in problem families in Cardiff. *British Journal of Delinquency*, 1958, 9, 95–101.

Witkin, H. A., Mednick, S. A., Schulsinger, F., Bakkerstrom, E., Christiansen,

K. O., Goodenough, D. R., Hirschhorn, K., Lundstein, C., Owen, C., Philip, J., Rubin, D. B., & Stocking, M. Criminality in XYY and XXY men. *Science*, 1976, *193*, 547–555.

Wolfe, M. The child's moral development. In K. R. Eissler (Ed.), *Searchlights on delinquency*. New York: International Universities Press, 1949, 236–272.

Wolfgang, M. E. (Ed.). *Crime and Culture*. New York: Wiley, 1968.

Wolman, B. B. Disturbances in acculturation. *American Journal of Psychotherapy*, 1949, *3*, 601–615.

Wolman, B. B. Hostility experiences in group psychotherapy. *International Journal of Social Psychiatry*, 1964, *10*, 55–61.

Wolman, B. B. *Children without childhood*. New York: Grune & Stratton, 1970.

Wolman, B. B. *Call no man normal*. New York: International Universities Press, 1973.

Wolman, B. B. Infantile autism. In D. V. Siva Sankar (Ed.), *Mental health in children*. New York: PJD, 1976, Vol. 2, pp. 599–612.

Wolman, B. B. (Ed.). *International encyclopedia of psychiatry, psychology, psychoanalysis, and neurology*. New York: Aesculapius Publishers, Inc., 1977.

Wolman, B. B. (Ed.). *Clinical diagnosis of mental disorders: A handbook*. New York: Plenum Press, 1978.

Wolman, B. B. (Ed.). *The therapist's handbook* (2nd edition). New York: Van Nostrand Reinhold, 1983a.

Wolman, B. B. Deculturation and disinhibition, In B. B. Wolman (Ed.), *International encyclopedia of psychiatry, psychology, psychoanalysis and neurology. Progress, Volume 1*. New York: Aesculapius, 1983b, pp. 82–86.

Wolman, B. B. *Problems of modern living: Psychology of adjustment*. Boston: American Press, 1984a.

Wolman, B. B. *Interactional psychotherapy*. New York: Van Nostrand Reinhold, 1984b.

Wolman, B. B. Intelligence and mental health. In B. B. Wolman (Ed.), *Handbook of intelligence*. New York: Wiley, 1985, pp. 849–872.

Wolman, B. B. The protoconscious and psychopathology. In B. B. Wolman & M. Ullman (Ed.), *Handbook of states of consciousness*. New York: Van Nostrand Reinhold, 1986.

Wolman, B. B., & Money, J. *Handbook to human sexuality*. Englewood Cliffs, NJ: Prentice-Hall, 1980.

Wolman, B. B. & Stricker, G. (Eds.). *Handbook of family and marital therapy*. New York: Plenum Press, 1983.

Yablonsky, L. *The violent gang*. New York: Macmillan, 1962.

Yudofsky, S., Williams, D., & Gorman, J. Propranolol in the treatment of rage and violent behavior in patients with chronic brain syndromes. *American Journal of Psychiatry*, 1981, *138*, 218–220.

Name Index

Agee, V.L., 104, 150, 166, 172
Aichhorn, A., 72, 98, 142, 144
Alexander, F., 143, 155
Allerton, R., 35
Allison, D., 72, 166
Anchor, K.N., 71
Andry, R.G., 33, 80

Bandura, A., 25, 33, 34, 35, 105, 106, 148
Barnhill, L., 165, 166
Barron, M.L., 31, 166
Bender, L., 100
Benedict, R., 17
Berkowitz, L., 30, 105, 106
Berman, S., 35
Bronner, A., 143
Brown, G.L., 13, 14

Callahan, E.J., 151
Campbell, M., 172
Carney, F.L., 157
Cazeneuve, J., 17
Christiansen, K.O., 7
Chwast, J., 143
Cleckley, H., 12, 96, 166
Cohen, A.K., 77
Crabtree, L., 173

Crain, W.C., 125
Cross, H.J., 71
Crowe, R.R., 7
Curry, J.F., 68

Dalamau, C.J., 143
Dietz, P.E., 172, 175
Dollard, J., 105
Douglas, P., 173

Eichelman, B., 138
Eissler, K.R., 99, 144, 177
Empey, L.T., 76
Epstein, E., 74
Erikson, M.L., 76
Eron, L.D., 125
Erwin, F.R., 15
Eysenck, H.J., 12

Fay, A., 147
Fields, W.S., 15, 17
Fookes, B.H., 151
Frank, S., 71
French, T.M., 155
Freud, A., 98
Freud, S., 5, 32, 58, 142
Friedlander, K., 33, 34

Gant, B., 165
Gibbens, T.C.N., 62, 69, 80, 170
Glover, E., 100
Glueck, E., 23, 69, 80, 95
Glueck, S., 23, 69, 80, 95
Goldstein, A., 167
Goldstone, S., 12, 151, 152, 174
Goodwin, F.K., 13, 14
Graham, J.R., 125
Greenacre, P., 99
Gualtieri, C.T., 139

Hamburg, D.A., 166
Hare, R.D., 7, 12, 13, 166, 174
Harmala, W., 72, 166
Hathaway, S.R., 125
Healy, W., 143
Hersov, L.A., 166
Hippocrates, 11
Hitler, A., 21, 53, 65
Hoffman, L., 30
Huesmann, L.R., 125
Huss, J., 50

Johnson, A., 35, 73
Jones, J.D., 172, 175, 177, 178
Julian, A., 167

Karpman, B., 97
Keith, C.R., 71, 160
Kempler, H.L., 125
Kernberg, P.F., 144
Khomeini, A., 65
Killman, P., 167
Klein, M., 102
Kohlberg, L., 69
Kostowski, W., 138
Krauss, B.J., 23
Krauss, H.H., 23
Kroptokin, P., 50

Lavin, G.K., 167
Lazarus, A.A., 146, 147, 148, 151
Lefkowitz, M.M., 67
Leitenberg, H., 151
Lejeune, J.V., 6
Leventhal, B.L., 137, 139
Levy, D.M., 23, 100
Lippitt, R., 30
Lippman, H.S., 101
Lombroso, C., 95
Loney, J., 68

Mahler, M.S., 102
Maj, J., 139
Makarenko, A.S., 183
Mannheim, H., 172
Mark, V.H., 15
Marshall, T., 78
Mason, A., 78
Masterson, J.F., 102, 144, 166
McCord, J., 95, 96, 170
McCord, W., 95, 96, 170
Mednick, S.A., 7, 14, 166
Mendel, G., 5
Mendelson, J.H., 13
Meyerhoff, R.G., 76
Meyerhoff, W.L., 76
Monachesi, E.D., 125
Money, J., 7
Monroe, R.R., 15
Moses, J., 6
Mosher, D.L., 71
Moss, G.R., 146, 147, 164
Moyers, K.E., 139

Nixon, R., 19

Ochberg, F.M., 16
O'Leary, K.D., 151
O'Neal, P., 7, 25

Parker, T., 35
Patterson, G., 165
Pincus, J.H., 13, 15
Pribram, K., 12

Quinlan, D.M., 71

Rada, R.T., 46, 172, 175
Rampling, D., 139
Ransford, H.E., 61
Reid, W.H., 12, 166
Rick, G.R., 146, 147, 164
Robin, A., 164
Robins, E., 68, 69, 125, 145
Robinson, S.M., 81
Rosen, S., 30
Rosenbaum, M., 165, 166
Ross, A.O., 105
Rugg, H.O., 19

Sadler, M., 138, 172
Sadoff, R.L., 23
Schalling, D., 7
Schmideberg, M., 100, 144

Name Index

Schwartz, A.H., 175
Scott, V., 125
Sears, R.R., 107
Shaffer, D., 166
Shapiro, D., 43
Smith, C., 71
Smoke, L., 151
Sorrels, J. Jr., 72
Spergel, L., 78, 81
Stanfield, S., 76
Stricker, G., 162, 164
Sullivan, H.S., 101, 102
Sweet, W.H., 15

Tharp, R.G., 149
Thompson, R.J. Jr., 68
Thrasher, F., 75, 81
Tinklenberg, J., 16
Trudeau, M., 166

Valzelli, L., 13

Walters, R.H., 25, 33, 34, 105, 106
Weinstock, M., 139
Weiss, C., 139
Wetzel, R.J., 149
Whyte, W.F., 75, 81
Williams, D.T., 139
Wilson, G.T., 151
Wilson, H., 31, 146, 148, 151
Witkin, H.A., 8
Wolfe, M., 33
Wolfgang, M.E., 166
Wolman, B.B., 6, 7, 23, 26, 43, 46, 71, 125, 130, 135, 162, 163, 164, 166, 168, 172

Yablonsky, L., 81, 83
Yudofsky, S., 139

Subject Index

Adolescents:
 delinquency, 73–86
 murderers, 71–72
 social factors, 69–72
Alcoholism, 16, 45–46
Ares, 44

Behavioral treatment methods:
 cognitive-behavior therapy, 149
 negative reinforcement, 149–150
 token economy, 149–150
 withdrawal, 150
Biochemical research
 amino metabolism, 14
 amphetamines, 14
 benzodiazepines, 14

Diagnostic and Statistical Manuals of Mental Disorders of the American Psychiatric Association:
 DSM-I, 87–88
 DSM-II, 87–89
 DSM-III, 47–48, 89–94, 123–124
Diagnostic methods:
 behavioral methods, 125–129
 DSM-III, 123–125
 sociodiagnostic method, 129–136
 testing, 125

Disinhibition and deculturation, 56–58
DNA, 5
Down syndrome, 6
Drug addiction, 16, 46–47

Ego, 49, 98–103, 118
Elizabethan Vagrancy Act, 171
Endocrinological research:
 minimal brain dysfunction (MBD), 14, 22
 prenatal factors, 14
 testosterone, 13
 XYY genotype, 13, 14
Eros, 44

Family psychotherapy, 162–165
Forced treatment, 172–174

Genetic research, 5–10
Goal-directed guidance (The Road to Life), 180–183
Group psychotherapy, 165–169

Hammer and anvil theory, 8–10
Homosexuality, 7
Hospitalization, 170–171, 174–179
Humors (Hippocrates), 11

Subject Index

Infantile autism, 5
"Innocent criminals," 41–42
Interactional psychotherapy:
  reality testing, 159
  the therapist, 157–158
  transference, 160–161

Juvenile delinquency:
  gangs, 80–83
  parental role, 79–80
  sex (gender), 75–76
  sociocultural factors, 73–75
  socioeconomic factors, 76–79

Klinefelter syndrome, 6, 8
Ku Klux Klan, 54

LSD, 26

Manic-depressive psychosis, 15, 23
Minimal brain dysfunction (MBD), 14, 122
Model Sentencing Act, 172
Moral issues:
  disinhibition and deculturation, 56–58
  moral crisis, 18–19, 21–22
  religion, 19–20
  sociocultural climate, 55–58

Nazism, 21, 43
Neurological research:
  brain damage, 122
  cortical maturation, 12
  EEG, 13
  lesions, 15
  lobotomy, 12
  reticular mechanism, 12
  seizures, 15

Parental influence:
  emotional deprivation, 22–34, 98–103
  socioeconomic factors, 23–25
  violent behavior, 35, 105–107
Pharmacological treatment, 138–141

Prisons. *See* Forced treatment
Protoconscious, 173
Psychoanalytic treatment methods, 142–145

Regimental Inmate Discipline Act (RID), 173
RNA, 5

Schizophrenia, 9, 15, 24, 173, 180
Sexuality:
  disinhibition, 44
  inhibition, 17
Sociocultural climate, 55–58
Soviet Revolution, 183
Suicidal danger, 49
Superego, 49, 98–103, 118, 142
Symptoms:
  and aging, 47
  alcoholism, 16, 45–46
  criminal behavior, 40–42, 67–83
  drug addiction, 16, 46–47
  hypochondriasis, 43–44
  lying, 44–45
  parasitism, 42–43
  sexual disinhibition, 44
  violent behavior, 49–55, 59–66, 73–83

Tay-Sachs disease, 6
Terrorists, 54, 180
Theories of sociopathy:
  behavioral, 104–107
  hyperinstrumental, 108–119
  other, 94–98
  psychoanalytic, 98–103
Treatment methods:
  behavioral treatment methods, 146–152
  family therapy, 162–169
  goal-directed guidance (The Road to Life), 180–183
  group therapy, 165–169
  interactional therapy, 154–161
  pharmacological methods, 137–141
  psychoanalytic methods, 142–145
  residential treatment, 170–179
TV violence, 60

About the Author

Benjamin B. Wolman received his Ph.D. from the University of Warsaw in 1935. During his distinguished career he has been: Chief Psychologist and Director, Mental Health Clinic, Tel-Aviv, Israel, 1935–1942; Director, Educational Services for Jewish Servicemen's Families in World War II, 1942–1945; Lecturer in Psychology, Teachers College, Tel-Aviv, Israel, 1945–1948; Visiting Lecturer, Columbia University, 1949–1953; Visiting Associate Professor of Psychology, Yeshiva University, 1953–1957; Clinical Lecturer in Psychiatry and Supervisor of Psychotherapy, Post Doctoral Program, Albert Einstein College of Medicine, 1958–1962; Clinical Professor in Psychoanalysis and Psychotherapy, Post Doctoral Program, Adelphi University, 1963–1965; Professor, Doctoral Program in Clinical Psychology, Long Island University, 1965–1978. Presently, he is Professor Emeritus, Long Island University, and has been in the private practice of psychoanalysis and psychotherapy since 1939.

Dr. Wolman is the author of over 200 scientific papers and 20 books in psychology and related fields. He is also the Editor-in-Chief of the *International Encyclopedia of Psy-*

chiatry, Psychology, Psychoanalysis, and Neurology. He is a Fellow of the American Psychological Association, American Sociological Association, and the Association for the Advancement of Psychotherapy, and President, International Organization for the Study of Group Tensions. Dr. Wolman is the recipient of the Dartmouth Medal of the American Library Association and of the Distinguished Contribution Award of the American Psychological Association.